KU-298-137

*With love to my
grandchildren
Jean, Donald and Andrew.*

LIST OF ILLUSTRATIONS

Robert F. Barclay

The Manse and the Mansion

Whittingehame Manse.

Finzean House.

W. M. Farquharson-Lang

The Manse and the Mansion

The Langs and the Farquharsons of Finzean 1750-1950

The Pentland Press Ltd
EDINBURGH

© W. M. Farquharson-Lang 1987
First published 1987 by
The Pentland Press Ltd,
Kippielaw, by Haddington,
East Lothian, Scotland.

All rights reserved.
Unauthorised duplication contravenes applicable laws.

Printed and Bound in Scotland by
D. & J. Croal Ltd, Haddington

ISBN 0 946270 40 6

CONTENTS

ACKNOWLEDGEMENTS

Researches into the history of a family have introduced to the writer a wide range of relatives and friends, some living as far distant as Carolina in the USA, South Africa and New Zealand, and all have generously provided material for this book. I am greatly indebted to them, particularly to Richard Hamilton, a distant cousin by marriage, who with his mother has traced the Lang ancestry and has produced genealogical tables of great value to a family historian; to Nan Roystone, now living in Washington, USA, with whom I share a great-grandfather and who knows more about the Farquharson family than most of us living in this country; to Graham Buchanan, a second cousin living in South Africa, who has provided valuable material on early Lang ancestry; and to my late sister, Laurina, who kindly allowed me to quote from the letters of our Uncle Norman.

The draft reminiscences of my father, sadly never completed, gave me an insight into his life and times and the early records of the Barony Church, Glasgow, lent me by Iain Crawford, the last Session Clerk of my grandfather's church, related to me the twenty-seven years of his ministry.

I am grateful too to the offices of the Church of Scotland for giving me access to Minutes of the General Assembly and to "the Fasti", the biographical records of ministers of the Church; to the Library of the University of Aberdeen, and, in writing the Farquharson chapters, to Finzean Estate for the full use of the Estate archives. Also my thanks to Manchester City Art Galleries for their permission to reproduce the Farquharson picture; *A Winter Morning*.

I have found valuable material in the following books:

The Private Papers of Anna Roberton Marshall.
Memories of John Marshall Lang by his wife.
J.G. Lockhart, *Cosmo Gordon Lang*.
Marshall B. Lang, *The Story of a Parish*.

Marshall B. Lang, *Whittingehame, the Seven Ages of a Parish.*
Robert Barclay, *Memories*, by his wife.
Robert Farquharson, *In and Out of Parliament.*
W.S. Swayne, *Parson's Pleasure.*
Kenneth Rose, *King George V* (Weidenfeld and Nicolson, 1983).

And for the encouragement of my wife and many others to get on with the work, I am much indebted.

Lastly my thanks to Barbara Rae for deciphering my illegible hand and producing a beautiful typescript and to Nancy Kellogg for presenting with such excellent skill the family trees of the Langs and the Farquharsons.

PREFACE

There is a great fascination in the unfolding history of a family, the same characteristics appearing in generation after generation, with many variations and the occasional brilliant exception. "The Manse and the Mansion" highlights the story of two interesting Scottish families, the Langs and the Farquharsons, made the more interesting by the contrast of their different dispositions and aptitudes. When, in June 1896, the author's father, Marshall Lang, married his mother, Norah Farquharson, the two families were merged.

In his short poem "Heredity", Thomas Hardy wrote:

> I am the family face:
> Flesh perishes, I live on
> Projecting trait and trace
> Through time to times anon,
> And leaping from place to place
> Over oblivion.

He could well have substituted family flair for family face.

In biographical sketches of his more prominent ancestors on both sides, Farquharson successfully evokes the family flair and the family traits. In the Lang family, from convenanting times, the most outstanding trait has been their deep concern for religion. Not all of them followed the traditions of Scottish Presbyterianism, and not all of them gave their services to Scotland, but over the years the contribution of the family as a whole has been to enrich the life of Scotland through their devotion to its religion. There was also an adventurous trait among the characteristics of the Langs, in their activities as well as in their thinking; this led some of them to pursue their careers in remote parts of the world. The Farquharsons, by contrast, were rooted in one place, their property in Finzean, Aberdeenshire; their flair was in the cultivation and improvement of their land and in playing their part in local affairs. There were exceptions, Farquharsons who gained a wider reputation, but for the most part their contribution to their times was through their services to their own locality.

The distinctive flairs of both Langs and Farquharsons live on in the descendants of Marshall Lang and Norah Farquharson.

ELSPETH DAVIES
(daughter of Patrick Keith Lang, 1863-1961)

(x)

1. INTRODUCTION

My father, Marshall Buchanan Lang, and my mother, Mary Eleanor Farquharson, were married at St. Bernard's Church, Edinburgh, on the tenth of June, 1896. My grandfather, John Marshall Lang, a former Moderator of the Church of Scotland, conducted the marriage ceremony and was assisted by Dr. George Matheson, the celebrated blind minister of St. Bernard's, and composer of the hymn, "Oh Love that wilt not let me go". My father had previously been an assistant to Dr. Matheson at St. Bernard's. The Rev. George Gillan, my granduncle and a son of a Moderator of the Church of Scotland, also took part in the service. My grandparents had certainly made sure that my father and mother were well and truly wed.

It was not a large and fashionable wedding. St. Bernard's is a small church on the north side of Edinburgh, only a short distance from my mother's home at 52 Inverleith Row where the reception was held. In keeping with the times the occasion was a display of fashion, no expense being spared in the purchase of the wedding gowns. *The Scotsman* reported the following day that my grandmother ("Grannie Farkie") was gowned in rich green corded silk, made in Louis Quatorze style, trimmed with Duchesse point lace and cream silk. Her green bonnet was decorated with Gloire de Dijon roses, and she carried a bouquet of the same flowers, adding in the report that "the presents, some of which were very costly, numbered nearly 200".

*   *   *

The occasion was more than the marriage of two persons; it had brought together two prominent Scottish families, the Langs and the Farquharsons.

Both were proud of their Scottish ancestry, having lived and been educated and for the most part practised their professions in Scotland, but in many ways the families were different. The Langs were a family, not a clan. They made no claim to the inherited ownership of property, nor were they attached to any particular part of Scotland. They had made their mark in their professions throughout the country as a whole, but probably more so in the cities of Scotland, in Glasgow and Aberdeen, in Dundee and Inverness.

Perhaps only Edinburgh escaped the attentions of my Lang forefathers although Whittingehame, only twenty miles from Edinburgh, was our family home for many years.

The Langs themselves were not a wealthy family although some of them acquired modest wealth through marriage. Many of them had been ministers and had large families. Their stipends alone could provide little more than the bare necessities of life but, by careful living and prudent management, their children were well cared for, well educated in Scottish day schools and many of them eventually became distinguished in their careers.

The Langs were a deeply religious family. From the sixteenth until the early years of the twentieth century they were fervently Presbyterian. My forebears, going back six generations in direct succession to the reign of Charles II, were zealous Covenanters and one, Adam Stobie, my great ($\times$ 4) grandfather, was imprisoned for singing the forbidden metrical psalms in the presence of the King's soldiers. He was placed on board a vessel for deportation to the West Indies but somehow managed to escape, and died peacefully at the age of 91 in his estate of Luscar, in the parish of Carnock, Fife.

Since the earliest days there have been many ministers from the Lang family in the Church of Scotland, four of whom have risen to the church's highest distinction as Moderators of the General Assembly. My father, one of the Moderators, was a staunch Presbyterian and jealously retained this branch of the faith in his family. It was his practice at the communion services he conducted to sing only the metrical psalms, a tradition handed down from the days of the Covenanters. My uncle Cosmo was the first of the family to complete his education outside Scotland and while studying law at Oxford changed course and trained for the priesthood of the Church of England, eventually to become the Archbishop of Canterbury. Once described as a deserter to Presbyterianism, a story is told that when he was at Canterbury, Cosmo received a telegram from the session clerk of Glasgow Cathedral, at that time without a minister, which read "Glasgow Cathedral now vacant. Return at once and all will be forgiven".

And yet with all their church connections, the Langs of the twentieth century could not be regarded as pious in the narrower sense of the word. My father's generation enjoyed the less serious side of life. They played games and fished, they had an endless supply of stories to suit nearly all occasions and even in their more mature years they were fond of playing practical jokes on one another.

Perhaps it was because they were too busy in their careers or caring for their families, or perhaps it was because they lacked the means to be trained, that no outstanding artistic talents seem to have developed in the Lang family. There were no musicians or artists or writers of note, but they had a sound appreciation of the arts. There were certainly distinguished preachers and orators in the family. Going back to my grandfather's generation, the male members of the family were blessed with rich and resonant voices put to full use in the pulpit or on the public platform or, in the case of Matheson Lang, on the stage. But surprisingly, and perhaps with some disappointment, none of them had more than the trace of a Scottish accent although they had all been educated in Scottish schools where a good Scots tongue would commonly be heard.

Born with good looks and a natural courtesy of manner, the Langs handed down from generation to generation the steadfast principles of their forefathers; they acquired ability and developed ambition. They were not perhaps the most brilliant of families, but they used to the full those qualities which contributed to their success.

*   *   *

Unlike the Langs, the Farquharsons were more a clan than a family, and laid claim to the occupation of land in Aberdeenshire by inheritance, continuously from the fourteenth century. However, it was not until the sixteenth century that the Finzean branch of the clan was established when Donald Farquharson, son of Finla Mor of Castleton of Braemar and bearer of the royal standard of Scotland at the Battle of Pinkie in 1547 where he was killed, acquired a small property, the lands of Tilliegarmond in the parish of Birse, in 1579.

Some thirty years later, Donald's younger brother, Robert, was granted by Charter from the Bishop of Aberdeen on 20th May, 1609, the lands of Finzean to which was added around 1628, the original property of Tilliegarmond. The estate gradually extended its boundaries by charter, by purchase, by inheritance through marriage, and sometimes in settlement of loans, until by 1814 the property of the laird of Finzean covered the largest area in its history, comprising the estate of Finzean in the Parish of Birse, a part of the Forest of

Birse, Lumphanan and Migvie, and Blackhall and Glendye in the Parish of Strachan.

For the next fifteen years the boundaries of the property remained unaltered until Blackhall and Glendye were sold in order to settle the debts of the laird of Finzean at that time. Lumphanan and Migvie and Finzean's share of the Forest of Birse were sold in 1936 to meet death duties following the death of Joseph Farquharson, RA. Since then there have been few alterations to the area and property of the estate.

The lairds of Finzean could not have been called wealthy although they owned property of considerable value. The income from the estate itself was usually just sufficient to maintain and modestly to improve the estate and at the best of times only small sums would go towards the personal uses of the laird. When a larger sum was required, property would have to be sold or the money would have to be borrowed. Unlike the families of many other Scottish lairds during the nineteenth century, the Farquharsons of Finzean had not amassed fortunes abroad or from the profits of industry at home, there being little or no money coming from outside the estate for its maintenance and improvement. But the Farquharsons lived comfortably and lacked little and most of the lairds managed to keep the property and their tenancies in good trim, to afforest the woodlands, to maintain the sporting interests, and to contribute generously to the welfare of their local community.

With one or two exceptions, the lairds of Finzean accepted their responsibilities as trustees of the land they had inherited. From the middle of the nineteenth century they attempted to move with the times, encouraging agricultural improvement and better forestry management. The laird provided more spacious farm houses and farm steadings and in co-operation with the tenants the drainage and productivity of their fields were greatly improved. The standard of housing of the smaller tenancies on Scottish farms at the beginning of the nineteenth century had been almost intolerable and Finzean was certainly no exception. There are still the remains of some of the old cottar houses on the estate showing that they were often little more than a small addition to the cowshed, consisting of one or two inadequate, mudfloored, thatched-roofed rooms where the tenant and his wife would bring up a large family of children. If there was any sanitation at all, it would be of the most primitive nature. Water would have to be carried from a nearby burn or well. Small wonder that under such conditions some of the children did not survive beyond infancy, and in every family there was the ever present dread of consumption. For the tenant himself there was insecurity, and sometimes more by ill luck than ill health he and his family would be evicted from the holding. In these early years the gulf between the laird and his tenants was wide. The relationship was one of master and servant and any understanding or sympathy for the conditions of the tenant and his family was unusual.

The middle of the nineteenth century brought changes. There was not only an industrial revolution; there was also a social revolution and a fierce agitation by workers against the hard conditions of their lives. Although these changes were more evident in the towns and cities of Scotland, they had not escaped the countryside and they had not escaped Finzean.

After more than half a century of neglect, the estate was badly run down. Providentially for Finzean, Dr. Francis Farquharson became laird in 1849. He had been a doctor in Edinburgh where he had himself witnessed the often fatal consequences of bad sanitation and housing and he was determined that such conditions should not be repeated on his estate. He borrowed a considerable sum of money, and during the latter half of the nineteenth century there were such improvements on the estate that the status and standard of living of the people rose beyond recognition.

Dr. Francis also brought to the estate a closer relationship between the laird and his tenants. As a medical practitioner in Edinburgh he had learnt to understand all classes of people and to appreciate their difficulties, and when he became laird he brought that understanding into the Finzean community. The folk at Finzean House did not flaunt their wealth because they had none to display. They were not ostentatious and they had no pride or vanity. During his lifetime and in the lifetime of his two sons, Francis moved amongst the people as one of them. As an old tenant once said to me, "The folk at the big hoos not only kent when the wife was going to have her baby, but they kent when the coo was going to have her calf".

Since the 1850s the Farquharsons of Finzean have been professional people, mainly doctors and bankers, and of course a professional artist of international repute. They handed on the estate in good shape, but by the nature of their occupations, the estate has never been supported by substantial wealth from outside sources used to increase its own intrinsic value.

Unlike the Langs, the Farquharsons could not boast of any strong church connections. Since the Finzean Farquharsons took no active part in the 1715 and 1745 rebellions, it would seem that they had Presbyterian sympathies. One of the lairds about that time was an elder of Birse church, perhaps some evidence that the family were Presbyterian during the rebellion. Later it seems likely that Dr. William Farquharson of Balfour, the father of Dr. Francis Farquharson of Finzean, was probably an Episcopalian as he was a kinsman of Bishop Skinner of Aberdeen. But in 1855 the name of Dr. Francis appears on the communion role of Birse church when there was perhaps a swing back to Presbyterianism. Before its renovation there was a substantial laird's pew in Birse church bearing the Finzean coat of arms. In 1863 Francis provided funds to build the present church at Finzean, at first a mission church of Birse, then a quoad sacra in 1903 and finally in 1926 the parish church of Finzean.

When they grew up, Robert and Joseph, the sons of Francis, seem to have little connection with any church, but when they were boys they regularly attended Birse Church with their father. In his old age Joseph used to speak about the services at Birse and how they went to hear the Rev. George Smith and how they waited every Sunday for the prayer, "All our righteousness is as filthy rags" causing suppressed and irreverent giggles in the laird's pew. The oldest inhabitants of Finzean record that in his latter years, Joseph seldom if ever went to Finzean church and there is no record of any connection with the neighbouring Episcopal churches. But their cousin, my maternal grandfather, William Walter Farquharson, was a staunch Episcopalian and was at one time secretary and treasurer of the Scottish Episcopal Church. When my grandfather married the daughter of Dr. Robert Gillan, the Moderator of the Church of Scotland in 1873, the balance of Presbyterianism and Episcopacy was restored.

The religious loyalties of the Farquarsons, not in any way causing division in the family, can best be represented by the generation of my mother (Mary Eleanor Farquharson, 1869-1953). There were four in the family — my Aunt Annie, a devoted member of the Church of Scotland if ever there was one and a member of St. Bernard's Church, Edinburgh, where she engaged in every church activity except the choir. She had no ear for music; indeed it used to be said in the family that she had difficulty in distinguishing between the national anthem and the Old Hundredth. Uncle Joe (laird of Finzean, 1935-1938) was no churchman; if anything he was Episcopal but he was really indifferent to religious affairs. My mother, like her eldest sister, was a keen member of the Church of Scotland, a tireless minister's wife and a proud Moderator's wife. The youngest member of the family, Aunt Angie, a special favourite of her Episcopal father, was a loyal Episcopalian all her life and at the age of 41 married William Shuckburgh Swayne (Uncle Toby) who became Bishop of Lincoln in 1920.

THE LANGS

1. The Langs and the Marshalls of Neilsland

The Langs came from Renfrewshire but little is known of their early history. At first of humble stock, their fortunes grew as the trade and commerce of the nearby city of Glasgow began to flourish and it is known that Robert Lang (1745-1795) was engaged in a successful merchant business trading with the West Indies. He lived in Paisley, the head of the firm by which he was employed being a certain Mr. Paisley. Robert's first wife (Rachel Inglis) had three children; Robert who died in infancy, and Elizabeth and Janet. Elizabeth married a cousin of her father's employer, another Mr. Paisley, by whom she had 16 children. When my father was Moderator of the Church of Scotland, he chose as one of his chaplains, Ninian Paisley, a descendant of one of the sixteen and, like my father, a great-grandson of Robert Lang.

Robert's second wife (Euphemia Morrison) also had three children (Gavin, John and Jane) and it is from Gavin that our branch of the Lang family stems.

Not yet 50 years of age and when young Gavin was only four, Robert was tragically killed in an accident to his coach on a bleak December morning on the road from Paisley to Glasgow, and thus ended at an early age a career of considerable promise.

Euphemia, now a widow, continued to live in Paisley where she brought up her family, the youngest, Jane, being born shortly after her father's death. Gavin Lang (1791-1869) did not pursue the business of his father, but chose to become a minister, the first of a succession of three generations who were ordained into the Church of Scotland. At first Gavin was appointed as assistant minister to the parish of West Kilbride, Ayrshire and it was there in 1829 when he was then 38 years of age that he met and married the truly remarkable Anna Roberton Marshall (1807-1886), a lady 16 years younger than himself and the daughter of John Marshall, the younger brother of David Marshall, the laird of Neilsland, a substantial property about three miles from Hamilton.

*　　　*　　　*

Any eccentricities in the Langs of the twentieth century can perhaps be traced back to Anna Roberton Marshall and her descendants. In contrast to the Langs of the nineteenth century, who seem to have been a fairly conventional branch of the family developing their trading interests carefully and with some success in Glasgow, the Marshalls were altogether more colourful; but when Anna Roberton's father married into the Stobie family, there was certainly much more to arouse the curiosity of a family historian. An extract of this branch of the family tree will clarify the relationship[1].

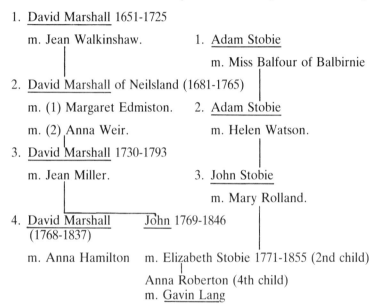

1. David Marshall 1651-1725

   m. Jean Walkinshaw.   1. Adam Stobie

                          m. Miss Balfour of Balbirnie

2. David Marshall of Neilsland (1681-1765)

   m. (1) Margaret Edmiston.   2. Adam Stobie

   m. (2) Anna Weir.   m. Helen Watson.

3. David Marshall 1730-1793

   m. Jean Miller.   3. John Stobie

                     m. Mary Rolland.

4. David Marshall   John 1769-1846
   (1768-1837)

   m. Anna Hamilton   m. Elizabeth Stobie 1771-1855 (2nd child)

                  Anna Roberton (4th child)
                  m. Gavin Lang

Records of the Marshall family before the seventeenth century have not been explored. The second and third David Marshall (see the extract of the family tree) were surgeons in the Royal Navy and it was the second David Marshall who acquired the fine agricultural and sporting property of Neilsland about the middle of the eighteenth century, thus establishing the Marshalls as a family of considerable

1. Most of the information about the Marshalls and the Stobies come from notes collected by David Marshall Lang (the eldest son of Anna and Gavin). These notes are now in the possession of Graham Buchanan, a great-great grandson of Gavin Lang.

influence in the county of Lanark for nearly one hundred and fifty years. The third David Marshall married Jean Miller, a young lady of renowned beauty and a daughter of the surgeon (general practitioner) of Hamilton. Their eldest son, the fourth David Marshall, was an entirely different character. In his early days, he had some business training in Glasgow, but his attempt to establish a small factory near Neilsland failed miserably. His interests were not in the making of money, but in its spending, living an extravagant and convival life with his aristocratic friends, hunting throughout the winter with the Duke of Hamilton and Lord Belhaven, and neglecting his estate throughout the year to such an extent that the impoverished Neilsland was sold some years after his death. It was through his hunting connections that he met his wife, Anna Hamilton, a remarkable lady who was a distant relative of the Duke. At the time there were many stories about the family of Anna Hamilton; her brother, James, was reputed to be the best speaker of Scots of his generation and, like the rest of his family, he was a generous and amiable companion, "a most convival and dangerous host, much coveted in these days, of enjoying his wine long after his guests had disappeared from the table or at least from sight". Another James Hamilton had been thrice Provost of Glasgow and yet another had married three times and had thirty legitimate children in his lifetime. But the fourth David and Anna Marshall were less fortunate and had no children.

David's younger brother, John, was a mild and indolent man who so mismanaged his own affairs that he was compelled to hand them over to his brother who in his turn squandered much of what he was supposed to protect. But John's place in the history of the family is not unimportant. He married Elizabeth Stobie, the daughter of a family whose strong convictions and often passionate behaviour at times led them into trouble. Nevertheless such characteristics must have had an influence upon the future generations of our family. John and Elizabeth had five children, the fourth being Anna Roberton Marshall, the future wife of Gavin Lang about whom more will be written later.

*   *   *

That part of the history of the Stobie family which is of interest here starts with drama and romance. Elizabeth's great-grandfather,

Adam Stobie, a young shoemaker who repaired the footwear of the folk at the laird's house, eloped with the daughter of the laird, Miss Balfour of Balbirnie, and married her. Their son, the second Adam Stobie, made good and became such a successful lawyer in Edinburgh that he was able to purchase for the family the estate of Luscar in Fife. They were a fervently religious family and it must have been one of the Stobies of an earlier generation who as a zealous Covenanter was imprisoned for singing the metrical psalms in front of the King's soldiers, eventually escaping before his deportation. In 1771, Elizabeth Stobie, the great-granddaughter of the romantic shoemaker, was born and in her life she became a notorious character, known for the violence of her temper and the intolerance with which she held her views. She completely dominated her husband, the spiritless John Marshall, and quarrelled incessantly with her brother-in-law, David, the laird of Nielsland. There had been family ructions ever since her marriage, which led to their daughter, Anna, leaving home to be adopted into the much more friendly household of David and Anna Marshall. The feud between the families culminated in a passionately held difference of opinion on one of those issues which can divide a family and a nation.

In 1843, the year of the Disruption of the Church of Scotland, Elizabeth gave her strong support to the Free Kirk of Scotland, thus antagonising herself to David who naturally supported the interests of "the Auld Kirk" and the lairdry. It was in this atmosphere of religious division before and after the historic days of the Disruption that Anna Roberton Marshall grew up, and it was then that she found her own deep convictions.

*   *   *

Anna kept a diary for over fifty years recording most of the events of her youth and much of her married life, but with the demands of her own family and the parish, and as she grew older, her records became more intermittent. Fortunately she has summarised much of her earlier years in a small booklet dedicated to her family and their descendants giving them a realistic picture of her life and an insight into her character.

In her childhood she was adopted and brought up by her uncle and aunt, the laird of Neilsland and his wife, as she had been, so she records, neglected in her own large family of which she was the youngest member. For many reasons the antagonism between Anna and her parents continued, a situation which brought additional unhappiness to her life. At about the age of twelve, the unexpected visit of a lady to Neilsland was to have a great influence on Anna and perhaps on the lives of some of her descendants. She not only taught Anna to read and sew but she introduced her to studying the Bible. Anna's uncle David, a wordly man who enjoyed the field sports of the neighbourhood and the company of his fellow lairds, found it difficult to understand Anna's devotions but he did not stand in her way and indeed encouraged her to attend a Sunday class. Increasingly she became deeply religious and was further inspired by the Rev. John Struthers, the minister of Hamilton, who had at one time been a cowherd on the Neilsland estate.

In his company she met many young ministers from nearby parishes and was particularly attracted by one, Gavin Lang, the assistant minister of West Kilbride. To quote her own words, she "looked favourably upon his attentions" and marriage was proposed, hardly in terms of the warmth and affection that might have been expected. Some years after her death, a letter from Gavin was found in Anna's jewel box, hidden behind her treasured possessions, a letter, brief, impatient and without any emotion, but historic in the annals of the Lang family.

"Dear Miss Marshall,
Would you be willing to become Mrs. Lang, and go with me to Nova Scotia?
An answer within two days will oblige.
Yours faithfully

Gavin Lang."

Her parents, her guardians and her family were united in their opposition to the marriage. In their opinion, Gavin was too old for her, he was an impecunious clergyman unable to support a wife in the style to which she was accustomed, and his prospects seemed to be uncertain to say the least, his immediate intention being to become a missionary in the New World. No doubt as laird of Neilsland her uncle and guardian, and even more so his wife, had other plans and hopes for a future alliance with a neighbouring county family. After great heart-searching and praying for divine guidance — probably for much longer than the specified two days —

Anna made up her mind and married Gavin at Neilsland on 15th July, 1829 "amid the tears of those present". Their tears were hardly dry before the family met again to say a sad farewell to Anna and Gavin as they sailed for Nova Scotia. Anna describes in her diaries the storms and dangers at the start of their voyage, and then the tedium of being becalmed before they reached Halifax after a journey of seven weeks. When they arrived they found the place was far from their expectations. Life was rough and for long periods Anna was left alone while Gavin pursued his missionary work into the interior. Anna became pregnant almost immediately after their arrival and in the absence of her husband found no comfort from the attentions of a drunken doctor. Life for her became almost intolerable; the strain had aroused the temper and impatience of her husband; her own health and the health of David, her first son, gave her much anxiety so that she more than welcomed the offer of her aunt and uncle to arrange and pay for the family's return home after an absence of about two years. Such was the unhappy start to a marriage which was to last for forty years.

*   *   *

On his return home Gavin had to wait before he was called to the charge of Glasford[1] in 1832 and there he remained as minister for thirty-seven years when he died in 1869. David, their eldest son, had been born in Nova Scotia; a year later a daughter was born at Neilsland before the family moved to Glasford and thereafter there followed, at little more than yearly intervals, ten more children, all born at Glasford. Invariably after the birth of each child poor Anna seemed to suffer ill health, often of a quite serious nature, but all her twelve children, except one, lived to a good old age[2].

The manse at Glasford, now a private house, was a substantial

1. The age-old name is correctly 'Glasford' with one 's'. When the railway company provided a station for the parish, they thought better and their sign-writer designated the parish 'Glassford' with two 's's'. However, the village is affectionately known locally as the 'Glassart'.
2. The children of Gavin and Anna Lang: David Marshall, 1830-1912; Anna Hamilton, 1831-1908; Robert, 1833-1835; John Marshall, 1834-1909; Gavin, 1835-unknown; Robert Hamilton, 1836-1913; Euphemia Morrison, 1838-unknown; Elizabeth Stobie, 1840-unknown; Jane, 1841-unknown; Margaret Wiseman, 1843-unknown; James Paisley, 1846-1929, Alexander, 1848-1930.

building but barely enough to accommodate the large family of Gavin and Anna Lang. At times the place would be filled to capacity with all the family at home and a few visitors to add to the numbers. But it was infrequent for the whole family to be in the manse at the same time as some of the older members had already left home before the younger were born. My grandfather, John Marshall, the fourth of the family, left home and became a student at Glasgow University at the age of 13, a year before his youngest brother was born.

Although the manse was often crowded, it was a happy home with plenty of activity and fun and family jokes, often at the expense of visiting ministers. Annual holidays for all the children together were out of the question, but a visit to Neilsland singly or in groups to stay with their uncle and aunt gave them greater freedom and much pleasure. They would play in the spacious garden and no doubt help themselves to the fruit from the carefully tended bushes and trees.

Anna was certainly the dominant member of the family, bringing up her children with affectionate understanding and teaching them at an early age to appreciate their duties in life, caring for those less fortunate than themselves. No one was a stranger at the manse and there was a welcome and hospitality for all. There would always be a pot of broth on the kitchen range and oatcakes on the girdle to sustain those who had travelled far and called at the kitchen door. It was a time of travelling people, often poverty-stricken Irishmen and their families seeking employment within the growing industrial prosperity of that part of Scotland, and if they found their way to Glasford, they would certainly be directed to the manse.

Future generations of the Lang family have much to be grateful for in their Marshall inheritance. Beyond anything else Anna was a God-fearing person, teaching and practising her strong Christian beliefs. She was at the same time a person of intelligent activity and purpose despite the fact that ill health dogged her throughout her life. She accepted infirmity bravely and quite naturally made for her family a very happy but simple home with much laughter and a constant exchange of friendly argument and chatter.

Less can be said of her husband, Gavin. He went his own way, diligently performing his duties as parish minister of Glasford, going his rounds mounted on his mare, Maggie, riding at a jogtrot to the furthest bounds of his domain. He visited every house regularly. He reckoned to know everyone whether they were his own folk or those of another denomination and this was important at a time of dissention in the Church. More successfully than many of his neighbouring ministers he managed to keep his congregation together, although some would leave him to travel three miles on a Sunday to the new Free Kirk at Strathaven.

Without much ambition he was happy to remain at Glasford throughout his ministry in Scotland. His sermons were always carefully prepared — woe betide the children if they made a noise outside his study on a Saturday — and were remembered by his congregation more for their length than for their inspiration. It is said of him that if he was not loved, he was greatly respected by his parishioners.

Gavin was less close to his family than Anna. There are hints that he was, like so many Victorian fathers, stern and remote from his children and at times there are indications of his quick temper. There may also have been a continuing tension between himself and the Marshalls at Neilsland who probably never accepted him warmly into their family circle since the early days when they had opposed his marriage to Anna.

Several of the twelve children of Gavin and Anna Lang became eminent in different fields, and others, if they did not themselves develop distinction, at least had the foresight to choose young men as husbands who in later life became distinguished. But that is another chapter in the history of the Lang family.

Gavin died at Glasford in 1869 and Anna in 1886 at Boswell, a nearby town, where she spent the latter years of her life. Both Gavin and Anna are buried in the churchyard at Glasford.

I

The Family of Gavin Lang 1791-1869 and (m. 1829) Anna Roberton Marshall 1807-1886

David Marshall 1830-1912 m. (a) Rosetta Fullerton Steven d. 1891 m. (b) Jessie A.R. Corbet d 1907 (The Senior Branch)	Anna Hamilton 1831-1908	Robert 1833-1835	John Marshall 1834-1909 m. Hannah Agnes Keith 1840-1921 (See II)	Gavin b.1835 m. Miss Corbet	Robert Hamilton 1836-1913 m. Margaret MacLennan

Euphemia Morrison b. 1838 m. Richard Stedman Cunliffe 1804-1879	Elizabeth Stobie b. 1840 m. Rev. Paton J. Gloag d. 1906	Jane b. 1841 m. (a) Mr Clarke m. (b) Rev. Alfred Maynard	Margaret Wiseman 1843-1909 m. Rev. John Pagan 1830-1909	James Paisley 1846-1929 m. Frances Anne Holbrow	Alexander 1848-1930 m. (a) Mary Dyckman m. (b) Mary Susan Keith

2. The Senior Branch

The eldest son of Gavin and Anna Lang was christened David Marshall (1830-1912) after his uncle, the laird of Neilsland. He was the first of five generations of the senior branch of the Lang family whose first-born up to the present day has always been named David Marshall. This followed the practice of four generations of the Marshalls of Neilsland to whom the name David had also been given to the eldest son. So that for nine generations and continuously from 1651 to the present day, the name David Marshall has been handed down from father to eldest son, except only in the case of the son of Gavin and Anna where succession was passed from uncle to nephew.

There were few opportunities for promising young men in the vicinity of Glasford so David sought a career elsewhere and went south eventually to become the manager of a large insurance company with London and Glasgow interests.

His son, the second generation David Marshall (1862-1946) first became a missionary in Japan with the Church Missionary Society, returning to England to become the rector of Fillingham, Lincolnshire, where he spent the rest of his life. He had two sons, David Marshall, the third generation, (1896-1978) and Charles Steven. After leaving school, David joined the army and served throughout the first World War. At the end of the War he returned to Cambridge to study medicine, and from there and later at Guy's Hospital, London, he qualified as a doctor, practising for most of his life in the south of England.

The eldest son of the doctor, David Marshall, was born in 1924 and became the fourth generation of the senior branch of the Lang family to bear the name. Ian Marshall, the second son of this generation, was born in 1928. After serving with the Intelligence Corps in World War II, David Marshall returned to Cambridge where he won high distinction as a student. This led to a short period of diplomatic service in the Middle East followed by an academic career which gained him an international reputation as an authority in Caucasian Studies. He held academic posts in St. John's College, Cambridge and the University of California, and in 1964 he was appointed Professor of Caucasian Studies in the University of London from which post he retired in 1984 after occupying the chair for over twenty years. His brother, Ian Marshall, the second son of this generation, was born in 1928. After his degree and a rowing "blue" at Cambridge, he followed a career in land management.

David's eldest son, the fifth generation to be named <u>David Marshall</u>, was born in 1957. Tragically, he was killed at the age of 19 while cliff climbing on the North Cornwall coast. David had a younger brother, Andrew Marshall, and two sisters, Caroline and Elizabeth.

3. The Family of Gavin and Anna Lang

Anna Hamilton (1831-1908) was the second child in the family of twelve of Gavin and Anna and, of the eleven surviving children, was the only one who remained unmarried. She had been very close to her mother throughout her life, helping her to bring up the large family — she was already 17 when her youngest brother was born — and she became fully involved in the active affairs of the manse at Glasford. As her parents grew older she looked after them and when her father died she and her mother moved to Boswell, at that time a quiet village near Glasford, where they lived for a number of years. Her final home for twenty-two years after the death of her mother was Stirling, where she interested herself in church and charitable work. She was known (to quote her obituary notice in the local newspaper) for "her sterling character, amiable disposition and many good works". She was buried beside her father and mother at Glasford where she had spent so many years of her life.

*   *   *

The third child, Robert, died in infancy (1833-1835).

*   *   *

The fourth child, John Marshall (1834-1909), my grandfather, was the most eminent of his generation and the father of a distinguished family. The next chapter is devoted to his life.

*   *   *

The fifth child, Gavin (1835-?) married a Miss Corbet in 1865 and they had seven children. Gavin followed his father into the ministry of the Church of Scotland, and in the year of his marriage was inducted to the parish of Fyvie in Aberdeenshire where he succeeded his elder brother, John Marshall. After he had been there for five years, he moved to Glasford where he succeeded his father as minister. The parish of Glasford was at that time within the patronage of the Earl of Eglington and Winton and it was he who appointed Gavin within a month of his father's death. It might seem at first that Gavin had benefited in his career by following in the footsteps of his elder brother and his father but he was beginning to feel that he could no longer live in their reflected glory, perhaps being reminded too frequently how the parishes had been run so successfully in their days. So very shortly after his induction at Glasford, Gavin made a bold move to get out of the family rut and accepted the challenging position of becoming the first minister of St. Andrew's Church, Montreal. From Montreal he moved to Inverness where he finished his ministry and earned for himself a reputation as a diligent pastor and a forceful preacher.

The eldest of his family, Gordon, became a doctor. His daughter, M'Ulaidh, married a doctor and their son, John Frew, also became a doctor — a refreshing departure from the traditional family profession of the church.

James (1874-1915) was the second son of Gavin, a captain in the King's Own Scottish Borderers in the First World War who was killed at Gallipoli in 1915, leaving a widow and one daughter.

Their third son, Alexander Matheson (1877-1948) became one of the leading actors of his time, After being educated at Inverness Academy and St. Andrews University where he showed more interest in the drama than anything else, he began a stage career with an apprenticeship in repertory. Later he joined Sir Frank Benson's Shakespearean Company where he had the unforgettable experience of acting with Lily Langtry and Ellen Terry, two of the greatest actresses of their time. Although he played most of the leading Shakespearean roles in the west end of London, he was perhaps best known for the parts of Mr. Wu and The Wandering Jew in the plays of those names. It was said by the kinder critics that his technique as an actor was perfect, no actor on the stage of his day having a wider command of expression in tone and gesture. It was the age of grand drama and Matheson provided it.

Later he undertook the dual role of actor-manager; in this he was less successful and it was sometimes said he was a poor judge of a play, and he had several failures. He later acted in a number of films, but he needed a live audience to inspire his talents. The screen was not his metier.

He married an actress, Hutin Britten, but there were no children. He died in 1948.

After Matheson, there followed four daughters, Mary, Annie, Jean and Phemie. Mary married Somerled Macdonald, the laird of Skeabost, Skye, but the other three sisters remained unmarried, continuing to live in Inverness for the rest of their lives. Like their grandmother, Anna, they were full of good works and were known within the family and to many in the North of Scotland as "the Miss Langs of Inverness".

*   *   *

The sixth member of the family, <u>Robert Hamilton Lang</u> (<u>1836-1913</u>), had a distinguished career in the Middle East. Educated in Scotland at Hamilton Academy and Glasgow University, his career began in Beirut when he was barely twenty years old and he worked continuously in Middle Eastern countries for the next 45 years. He was a contemporary of Lord Cromer, the founder of Modern Egypt, and one of a small band of Britishers who at that time gave the best part of their lives to guide and assist the emergence of Middle Eastern countries into their modern role as free nations. He had all the qualities required to deal with the intricacies of the Middle Eastern political scene. He was patient and tactful, clear and exact in his judgements, understanding and sympathetic towards the most complex and devious situations, and was supported by a fluent knowledge of Arabic and other languages of the Middle East. It was no surprise to those who knew him that his career advanced rapidly from a commercial post in Beirut to a position of great responsibility in the developing government of Egypt.

After Beirut he moved to Cyprus where he started the first bank on the island, a branch of the Imperial Ottoman Bank. At a time of a world shortage of cotton caused by the American Civil War, he was asked to encourage cotton growing in Cyprus. When he saw there was a lack of response by the local inhabitants, he started his own farm of 800 acres and so successfully cultivated a crop that others followed his example. He lived like a patriach, helping the simple peasantry to cope with their problems: shortage of water, plagues of locusts, famine, and not least the iniquities of usury. So varied and so successful were his activities that he was appointed British Consul in Cyprus at the age of 35. There his influence was long remembered, when many years later a thoroughfare in Larnaca was named "Lang Street" in recognition of his services.

The basis of his work had always been the Imperial Ottoman Bank. After establishing a branch of the bank in Cyprus at an early age, he was transferred to Egypt to attempt to unravel the affairs of the bank during the difficult times of the spendthrift Khedive Ismail. It would be about this time that he met Sir Evelyn Baring (Lord Cromer) while assisting him to settle the repayment of the huge Egyptian public debt. He was now becoming an authority on international debt affairs and was shortly to become involved in the settlement of the foreign debts of Turkey. He created a new Ottoman Administration so successfully that Turkey was raised to solvency in a comparatively short period.

At the age of fifty, after years of strain, he had every intention of retiring and had actually returned to England where he had bought a house in Constable's corner of Essex hoping to enjoy a more leisurely life with his wife and young family of one son and three daughters.

When he was forty, Robert had married the daughter of a Scottish laird, Margaret MacLennan of Blairvaddich, a talented young lady much younger than himself. They had four children. The eldest, <u>Anna Hamilton</u> (<u>1880-1964</u>) married the Rev. Richard de Crespigny Thelwall, latterly of St. Oswald's Church, Birmingham. They had seven children, two boys who both went into the church, and five girls. The second, <u>Mary Alice</u> (<u>1883-1976</u>) married an American, Peter Bryon Rogers of the American Navy. She settled in the States, had two sons and seldom returned to the country of her birth. The only son, <u>Walter Hamilton</u> (<u>1884-1939</u>) a colonel in the Indian Army, married three times. His third wife, Ruby Harris Davis, came from New Zealand and was much younger than him, surviving him by thirty-seven years. After his death, she lived in London, keeping in touch with some of her Lang relations. She died in 1976. Unfortunately, there were no children from his three marriages to carry on this distinguished branch of the family. The youngest member of the family, Victoria Maggie (1886-1984), known to us all as "Queenie", continued to live in Farnham, Surrey, until her death at the great age of ninety-eight. She was sixty-three when she married Hamilton Hofman Scott, a London stockbroker, whom she had known almost since her childhood, and for fifteen years in their old age they enjoyed a blissfully happy life together.

But spending time with his family and hopes of retirement were not to be realised. Robert was shortly recalled to Cairo to represent the British Government and international financiers in the management of the Estates of the late Khedive Ismail (the Daira Sanieh), a vast area of nearly half a million acres with its own railway and river vessels and employing nearly 9000 Egyptians. The huge deficit which the estates had inherited when Robert Hamilton Lang, together with a French controller, took over, showed in time a credit and when he finally retired from Egypt in 1896, the administration effected a credit of no less than £438,000 annually to the Egyptian budget.

Towards the end of the century, he again indicated a wish to retire, but the demands for his services and perhaps his own desire to be more fully occupied and return to the Middle East were so pressing that although now over sixty years of age, he returned to Constantinople as Director General of the Imperial Ottoman Bank. For Robert Hamilton Lang the couplet of Rudyard Kipling was very true:

"If you've heard the East a'calling
You won't ever hear aught else"

He retired finally in 1902 and, although he continued to sit on the Council of the Bank in London, he had at last ample time to enjoy the beauty of his home in Essex. He died in 1913.

A paragraph from his obituary notice in *The Times* sums up the success of this outstanding man:

"His character was remarkable by the adaptation of his intense British thoroughness to the ways of the East. He was a born diplomatist and his smiling and patient tact won a way for him through tiresome labyrinths of Oriental intrigue. He learned the working of the Eastern mind as few Britons have."

He was made a CMG in 1896 and a KCMG in 1897 and also received the highest decorations from the countries in which he served.

*   *   *

The first six children of Gavin and Anna had been five boys and one girl. As if to redress the balance there followed four daughters, Euphemia, Elizabeth, Jane and Margaret.

At the age of twenty four, <u>Euphemia Morrison</u> (<u>b. 1838</u>) married

Richard Stedman Cunliffe[1] (1804-1876) who was born in Leipzig and was living there in 1813 at the time of Napoleon's decisive defeat in that city. The occupation of his father and the reason why the family were living in Leipzig at that time are not known, but it is known that in later life Richard Stedman returned to Glasgow to become partner in one of the leading shipping firms in that city, Randolph Elder and Company, a firm more recently to become associated with Fairfield Shipbuilders. In his business Richard acquired a considerable fortune which enabled him generously to contribute to the charities of Glasgow, and his son also donated handsomely towards the building of the new Barony Church in Glasgow, built during the ministry of his brother-in-law, John Marshall Lang. There is a beautiful chapel in the Barony, presented by their son, dedicated to the memory of Richard Stedman Cunliffe and his wife Euphemia Lang.

Their son, also Richard Stedman Cunliffe (1870-1932) retained a close friendship with his Lang relations, particularly with my uncle and his cousin, Patrick Keith Lang.

Richard was a man of great ability. Professionally he was a solicitor in Glasgow, held in the highest esteem as one of the most prominent lawyers in Scotland. But he was also an eminent scholar and wrote two great dictionaries, the *New Shakespearean Dictionary* and the *Lexicon of Homeric Dialect*. For his contribution to British scholarship he was awarded an honorary Doctorate of Laws by his Alma Mater, Glasgow University.

As a lexicographer, Dr. Samuel Johnson used to describe himself as "a harmless drudge"; Richard Cunliffe was certainly not that. He was a man full of humour and, as was not unusual with the Victorians of the time, enjoyed playing practical jokes especially on his cousin, my Uncle Patrick, jokes often so elaborate that they have become legendary in our family. He was fond of children and joined naturally in their games, his frequent visits to the Patrick Lang's Surrey home always being particularly popular with the children who welcomed him as "King Richard".

*   *   *

Elizabeth Stobie Lang (1840-1914) was twenty-seven when she

---

[1] The name can be spelt with or without the terminal "e". Baptism certificates give the name as Cunliff but Cunliffe has now become the more common spelling.

married the Rev. Paton Gloag, at that time the minister of Blantyre, Lanark, a man seventeen years older than herself. He was a prolific writer of theology and perhaps contributed more to the church as a scholar than as a parish minister. His academic distinction was readily recognised. He had the honour to be selected as Baird Lecturer, he was a Doctor of Divinity of St. Andrews University, a Doctor of Laws of Aberdeen University and was elected as Moderator of the General Assembly of the Church of Scotland in 1889. After a short period as a Divinity Professor in Aberdeen, Paton Gloag retired to Edinburgh where he died in 1906 at the age of 83. Elizabeth survived him by eight years. They had no children.

*   *   *

Less is known of <u>Jane Lang</u> (<u>b. 1841</u>). Unlike her two sisters, her two husbands were not prominent in any walk of life. When she was twenty-one, she married a Mr. Clarke and some years after his premature death she married again, this time an English Church clergyman named Alfred Maynard.

*   *   *

<u>Margaret Wiseman Lang</u> (<u>1843-1909</u>) the youngest of the five daughters of Gavin and Anna, at the age of twenty-seven married another distinguished minister of the Church of Scotland, the Rev. John Pagan (1830-1909). After a short ministry in Forgandenny in Perthshire, John Pagan was translated to the parish church of Bothwell near Hamilton in 1865 and there continued as minister for the rest of his life, a period of forty-four years. In contrast to his brother-in-law, Dr. Paton Gloag, John Pagan was not a scholar; he was an indefatigable worker in his parish, tending his flock, restoring the ancient and historic church of Bothwell and finding time to be convener of the two most important committees of the church, one charged with the responsibility of its missions and the other with that of its finances. In recognition of his services he was made a Doctor of Divinity of Glasgow University and was elected Moderator of the General Assembly in 1899.

John and Margaret Pagan had four children. The two elder boys both became ministers, the first, John Hamilton, a minister in Kimberley, South Africa, where he had emigrated on grounds of ill-health and where he died of consumption at the age of forty-two.

Gavin Lang, the second son, was a remarkable man. At the age of thirty-eight, he was chosen to be minister of St. George's, Charlotte Square, one of the most influential churches in Edinburgh, and at the time there seemed every prospect that he would follow in the footsteps of his distinguished father and uncles. At the outbreak of war in 1914, Gavin felt compelled to take an active part in the war and sought permission from his kirk session to join the forces. They readily agreed to let him go and to keep the charge vacant for his return. At the age of 42 he joined up and became a private in the Royal Scots, was rapidly promoted to the rank of Captain, was awarded the MC, and at forty-four was killed leading his men into action in a wood outside Arras in April, 1917. There is a memorial to Gavin Lang Pagan in the Crypt of St. Andrew's and St. George's Church, Edinburgh, the church which now unites his old church with the neighbouring church of St. Andrew's. He married Mabel Douglas in 1915.

The third son of John and Margaret Pagan, Alexander Hamilton, farmed and died in South Africa and their only daughter and youngest of the family, Anna Marshall, died unmarried.

*   *   *

After a succession of four daughters, the score in the family of Gavin and Anna stood at five all — five sons and five daughters. But in the end, the boys were to win, with the births of two sons, James Paisley and Alexander, thus completing the family of twelve, seven boys and five girls. Gavin was in his fifty-eighth year when Alexander was born and Anna was forty-one, having given birth to twelve children in nineteen years.

James Paisley Lang (1846-1929), a sixth son, was ordained as a minister of the Church of Scotland at the age of twenty-one and shortly afterwards went to India as a missionary, where he served for eleven years before returning to Scotland. In his mid-thirties he was appointed minister of the East Church, Stirling, where he continued for many years as a much beloved and celebrated pastor. While he was in India, he married Frances Anne Holbrow, the daughter of a colonel in the Indian Army. They had three daughters and one son, George Holbrow Lang, who became an officer in the Royal Navy and was decorated for distinguished service in the 1914-18 War. His son, Ian, followed his father as a naval officer and served at sea towards the end of the second World War. The youngest daughter, Anna, married James Taylor, a doctor in Dunkeld. Both Anna and James were more to our family than rather distant relations; they were very close friends of my parents. James and my father would spend many hours together, walking, talking, and exchanging endless stories, oft repeated as they grew older, while Anna, less easy to talk to as she was so deaf, was always a great help to my mother in the house and frequently came to the rescue when there were domestic crises.

*   *   *

Alexander (1848-1930), the twelfth and last child of Gavin and Anna, like the rest of his brothers and sisters was brought up in the manse of Glasford, continuing his education in Glasgow and at the University. He married first an American lady, Mary Dyckman, by whom he had one daughter, but Mary died at an early age after five years of marriage. Some years later, he married Mary Susan Keith, the younger sister of my grandmother (Grannie Lang — the wife of John Marshall Lang). They had three children, one son and two daughters. Their son, Leslie Lang, had a distinguished career in the Church of England, becoming Bishop of Woolwich at a young age and later Assistant Bishop and Archdeacon of Winchester. Their youngest daughter, Naomi (1891-) was unmarried and was for many years curator of Thomas Hardy's birthplace near Dorchester. At the age of 95 she continues to live in the South of England.

Alexander followed a successful career in commerce and banking, mainly in Canada and the United States, becoming London manager of the Bank of Monteal in 1863, and for his services to international banking he was awarded the CMG. Enjoying a long and happy retirement in good health, Alexander and Mary continued to live in London and became very much the centre of the family, south of the border, until they died within a year of one another in 1930/31.

4. John Marshall Lang CVO, DD, LL D

One of the most treasured possessions of our family is a Scottish silver loving cup, presented to my grandfather, John Marshall Lang, in recognition of some special service he gave to the Church of Scotland. On the cup there is inscribed a tribute to his ability, his kindness and his courtesy, qualities he had in such measure that he is recognised by many of us as the most distinguished and beloved member of our two families.

The Very Rev. John Marshall Lang, D.D.

John Marshall Lang (1834-1909) — Grandfather Lang — was born in the manse of Glasford within a year of his brother, Robert. He is reported to have been a strong lusty boy who more than held his own with his brothers and sisters and would probably have been the leader in many of the rowdy games played in the spacious gardens of the manse. On a small stipend and probably with little support from Anna's family at Neilsland, the standard of living was inevitably frugal, but the house was well managed by Anna and she made sure that their young lives were happy. Gavin allowed the house to be run by Anna and stood apart from the activities of the young members of his household. The daughter of a laird, Anna had of course to keep up appearances and no doubt it was her wish that her children should be educated privately and not have to rub shoulders with the children of the farm servants and weavers of Glasford. A room was acquired in a neighbouring building for use as a classroom for the Lang family, and a tutor engaged. There would have been several reasons for the quick succession of tutors through the classroom at Glasford, but it seems likely that these lowly-paid, untrained and inexperienced, timid young men were no match for the boisterous behaviour of the young Lang family. My grandfather recalled that he had had five tutors during his time who had failed to give him a satisfactory education. The result was that all the Lang boys had to finish their education at this stage by going to schools in Glasgow to bring them up to a reasonable standard. My grandfather went for one year to the Glasgow High School and his younger brother Robert to Hamilton Academy. It was a long trek from Glasford to Glasgow every day, six miles by horse-drawn coach or on foot to Hamilton, or if they were lucky thumbing a lift on a farm cart, and then for the rest of the journey on the new railway from Hamilton to Glasgow.

At the age of thirteen John Marshall was enrolled as a student of Glasgow University. No written examination had to be passed at that time, the test for admission being the result of the careful scrutiny of each applicant by the professors of Latin and Greek, and the payment of the fee. A red gown having been purchased and satisfactory lodgings engaged, the youthful John Marshall embarked upon an academic career of four years, studying Latin and Greek and the philosophies in order to get his first degree as Master of Arts, to be followed by three years in the Divinity Hall to gain the second degree of Batchelor of Divinity. But it was not all work. He seems to have taken a full part in university life, enjoying parties with his fellow students, speaking at the debating society where he developed his powers of oratory, and, although no party politician, joining vigorously in the grand fights promoted by the Conservatives and Liberals at the Rectorial Elections.

*   *   *

He was licensed to preach at the age of twenty-one and a year later was ordained by the Presbytery of Aberdeen as a minister of the Church of Scotland. He was now a young man of considerable presence and good looks with a confidence and manner beyond his age and it was not long before he was invited to become minister of the East Church (St. Nicholas), Aberdeen, a charge of responsibility which proved to be somewhat beyond his experience. He entered into his new appointment with an enthusiasm of youth which was not always shared by the Presbytery of Aberdeen. It had been the custom of the Church of Scotland for the congregation to stand during prayers and to sit during praise. John Marshall persuaded his congregation to reverse the practice and although this was acceptable to his people, and only a few years later became common throughout the church, it was certainly not acceptable to the Presbytery who firmly told him and his congregation to sit down. He was in advance of his time and, while the Presbytery treated him kindly, they were firm in their resolution not to change their ways at the suggestion of a youthful colleague straight out of college.

He had only been two years in Aberdeen when a parish, more suitable for a young minister, fell vacant. The minister of Fyvie had died the day after John Marshall had met Colonel Cosmo Gordon of Fyvie, the patron of the living. The colonel had heard of the young man, was greatly impressed on meeting him and offered him the charge. It was some time before John Marshall made up his mind, but a spell of ill-health decided matters for him and he accepted the invitation. His six years at Fyvie were full of happiness and promise. Here he had time to find his feet as a parish minister; like his father before him he visited his parishioners, he preached to large and appreciative country congregations, not only in his church but in farm barns in the more remote parts of the parish, where the older folk would sit on boards and barrels while the farm lads perched on the rafters dangling their feet above his head as he preached to them.

In 1861 John Marshall married Hannah Agnes, the daughter of the Rev. Dr. Peter Hay Keith, minister of Hamilton, and within a year of their marriage, Gavin Douglas was born. From notes written by my grandmother recording the progress of her children, it seems that young Gavin enjoyed perfect health for nearly four years but he was said to have had an unusually restless nature. To the great grief of his parents he died of whooping cough shortly after they left Fyvie. Two more boys were born while they were at Fyvie, Patrick Keith and Cosmo Gordon, the latter named after the laird of Fyvie[1].

In 1864, Dr. Norman Macleod, the celebrated minister of the Barony Church, Glasgow, wrote to my grandfather asking him if he would become the first minister in a new church in the Anderston district of the Barony Church. He would be responsible for establishing a new congregation and initiating all the work in the church and parish. The population of the Barony parish had increased so greatly that it was thought that an extension to the existing church should be formed. In accepting the invitation and the challenge, there began for my grandfather a long connection with the Barony Church. He quickly realised that in order to attract a working class congregation, there would have to be innovations in the traditional church service. An organ was introduced — the first in the Church of Scotland — and the conduct of church worship was made more friendly; services were altogether briefer and brighter, and quickly attracted good congregations. During his ministry at Anderston he began a long association with civic work in Glasgow and while he was there he greatly assisted the medical officer of health to control a threatened outbreak of cholera.

My grandparents were only four years at Anderston but during that time there were two additions to the family, Douglas Hamilton, and my father, Marshall Buchanan.

Morningside, Edinburgh, was the next move of my grandparents, my grandfather being inducted to the charge in 1868. At that time Morningside was still a quiet country village but the suburban railway to Edinburgh was attracting the development of a well-to-do community, and the building of large houses. In order to

---

1. My grandparents had eight children: Gavin Douglas 1862-1866; Patrick Keith 1863-1961; Cosmo Gordon 1864-1945; Douglas Hamilton 1866-1945; Marshall Buchanan 1868-1954; Hannah Buchanan 1872-1952; Norman Macleod 1875-1956; David Marshall 1876-1925.

accommodate the increasing population of the parish, my grandfather built a large addition to the existing church and rearranged and decorated the interior, adding much to the beauty of its style.

Although my grandfather was greatly beloved by a congregation of thoughtful, cultured and successful business and professional people, he felt that his mission was in other spheres. Perhaps to offset the endless round of tea parties and charitable functions in Morningside, he took an increasing active part in church organisations in Edinburgh and was chosen to represent the church at a Presbyterian Assembly in America, the first of many foreign visits which he greatly enjoyed. But he wanted to return to more active parochial work and when the great Dr. Norman Macleod of the Barony died in 1873, he readily accepted the invitation to succeed him.

The only daughter of their family of eight, Hannah Buchanan, was born at Morningside.

5. The Barony

On a bleak January day in 1873, the Lang family moved from the manse of Morningside to 5, Woodlands Terrace, Glasgow, where they were to live for twenty-seven years during my grandfather's ministry at the Barony Church. There were now five children in the family; Patrick was ten years of age and the youngest child, Hannah, was only four. During their early years in Glasgow, two more boys were born, Norman Macleod (named after my grandfather's distinguished predecessor at the Barony) in 1875 and David Marshall in 1876.

Norman Macleod had been minister of the Barony for twenty-one years, a great preacher and a beloved pastor, but my grandfather, now in the prime of life at thirty-nine years and entering upon his new charge with great vision and determination, was soon to discover that there was much to be done in this predominantly working-class parish. The capacity of the church was limited and the fabric was showing signs of wear and tear; church membership was small in relation to the growing population, and church attendance seemed to come more from the well-to-do section of the society rather than the working folk. He soon realised that a new church with a new approach was needed. It would normally have been the duty of the heritors to provide a place of worship in the parish, but the heritors were many and some not particularly interested in the affairs of the church. Knowing that there would be endless wrangling and probably a second-rate building at the end of the day, my grandfather decided to embark upon the planning and building of a new church from funds to be raised from the congregation and the public outside the parish, and from the larger and interested heritors. The church was built in a few months over two years and was dedicated in April 1889, a magnificent building of notable height with fine high arches, to have a seating capacity for 1100. The old church had once been described by Dean Stanley as "the ugliest church he had ever seen except one". The new Barony was acknowledged as "one of the noblest sanctuaries to be found anywhere". The completion of the church was not the end of my grandfather's worries as there was a considerable debt to be paid off, but by constant appeals and from the proceeds of a most successful bazaar, the debt was finally settled. The Cunliffe Chapel in the Barony, presented by their son in memory of Richard Stedman Cunliffe and his wife,

Euphemia Lang, a younger sister of my grandfather, is one of the beautiful features of the building.

When my grandfather went to the old Barony Church in 1873, the payment of rent for seats in the church was practised, common at that time in most of the city churches in Scotland and frequently a question debated in the General Assembly of the Church. My grandfather disliked this division of his congregation whereby those who could afford to pay seat rents sat in the body of the kirk while those who could not or would not, sat in the gallery. He also objected in his country parishes to the custom of the farmer and his family sitting in the pew directly in front of his farm servants and their families. In the new Barony Church, there were to be no seat rents, it was to be a free and open church. "Poverty need be no exclusion to the House of God" wrote my grandfather in the Barony Report of 1889.

His reputation as a preacher was well established before he came to the Barony. In Glasgow he continued to draw large congregations every Sunday, especially at his evening services where the younger people would queue outside, waiting to be admitted to the church. It was a time of great preachers and Marshall Lang was one of them. Today his sermons would be regarded as too long and often too dramatic and evangelical but they always had a clear and straightforward message which went direct to the hearts of the people of Glasgow.

During his ministry at the Barony the membership of the church increased steadily, reaching a figure of 2292 in his last year[1]. It had been his aim to visit every parishioner once every two years but with other demands on his time and the increase in numbers he found it impossible to do so, In addition to all this, with the assistance of his elders and a junior minister, there were many church activities to organise, my grandmother giving him devoted assistance, particularly in looking after the women's and children's interests in the parish.

To express their appreciation for his arduous and successful work at the Barony for twenty-five years, the congregation entertained my

1. Sadly, in 1985 the congregation of the Barony Church was dissolved because of a fall in membership in a much depopulated area of Glasgow but happily the splendid building has now been taken over by Strathclyde University as a ceremonial hall, a fitting use for a building founded by a former minister of the church who became the Principal of a Scottish University.

grandparents in 1898 to "a monster soiree" (so named by the Session Clerk) in the St. Andrews Halls, Glasgow. To the disappointment of all his friends he had refused to accept a gift to commemorate the anniversary but he expressed the wish that the funds should be used to clean and decorate the church, something that was already necessary although the building, situated as it was in the midst of industrial Glasgow, was only ten years old. But the warmth of their regard and their affection for my grandparents were expressed in glowing tributes, to them more valuable than any silver token. The family had taken their part in the work of the church; in the early days while they were at home, Patrick and Cosmo both helped in its activities, Douglas was a lieutenant in the Boys' Brigade, Marshall, as a student, took services in the Canal Street Mission, Hannah helped in the Girl's Recreation Institute, no doubt encouraged to attend as the assistant minister at the time, Robert Barclay, eventually became her husband, and Norman, still a schoolboy, is listed among those who contributed to the church.

As the minister of a great industrial parish in Glasgow, Marshall Lang was inevitably associated with the public work of the city and was deeply interested in all movements for the social improvement of the people. He was on the School Board for nine years and on one occasion headed the poll at the election, a matter of great significance in those days. He was a member of a committee appointed by the Town Council to report on the housing of the poor of Glasgow and for many years was chaplain to the 1st Lanark Volunteers, later to become part of the territorials of the city. When he left in 1900, the citizens of Glasgow made a presentation to him "in recognition of his eminent public service and as an expression of the esteem and affection in which he is held".

In the wider work of the church, my grandfather somehow managed to find time to play a major part. He was elected president of an international body, the Council of Reformed Churches, which took him to meetings in Europe, Australia and America; he was Chairman of a Committee on the Religious Condition of the People of Scotland which reported to the General Assembly in 1896 after six years of study, and his crowning achievement was his election to the Moderational Chair of the General Assembly in 1893.

*   *   *

There have been many ministers in the Church of Scotland who have dedicated themselves to improving the social conditions of the people, whose humanitarian concern was a stamp of their religious piety. During the last quarter of the nineteenth century my grandfather was one of the most prominent of these ministers. At the Barony he had access to the problems of a working class community. He was privileged to visit people in their homes and see for himself their living conditions. He visited their schools and hospitals. He understood the terms of their employment and was well aware of the evils of the time, of intemperance and gambling. And he took every opportunity to present these problems to the people of Scotland on the frequent occasions he was invited to speak, notably when he delivered the Duff lectures, in his closing address to the General Assembly as its Moderator and when he presented to the Assembly the Report of his Commission on the Religious Condition of the People of Scotland.

He frequently spoke of the contrast of wealth and poverty. True, Glasgow had flourished in the nineteenth century, but there were zones of wealth and zones of poverty, a great division which seemingly could not be bridged. Insecurity of employment was a major problem of his time in Glasgow. Workers would be paid on and paid off at the whim of the employer or of his more ruthless steward, or a glut of work would be followed by a famine of employment. At the Assembly he commended the earnest effort of the people of Scotland to realise a better distribution of wealth and more equitable adjustments in conditions. He spoke in support of the co-operation of workers, no doubt having in mind the rise of the trade union movement at that time, and said "On placing wages on a surer footing, the union has blessed society in general". But almost prophetically he warned of the dangers of overstepping the mark by so rigorously advocating the cause of the tradesman that the trade itself might be injured.

The housing of the people in his parish and elsewhere became his special interest. While he recognised improvement, particularly in some mining areas, he deplored the degrading conditions of others with inadequate water and shared sanitation, and in rural areas he was critical of many of the farm bothies which he described as dreary and unnatural and regarded with indifference by the farmers. He deplored intemperance and its consequences upon family life but blamed the social circumstances of the time which drove many men and women to break the monotony of their lives "in the noisy mirth of the public house".

In submitting their Report to the General Assembly on the Religious Condition of the People, my grandfather's Commission had collected evidence from presbyteries throughout Scotland. They spoke of the fishermen of Scotland as being "kindly, hearty, impulsive folk with a deep current of religious earnestness" and of farm workers as "mainly self-reliant, industrious and sober". They analysed the perennial problem of declining church attendance and blamed the increase of Sunday labour, more amusements and Sunday visiting as causes. "Saturday night revelling", they said, "discourages Sunday morning attendance". And of the modern transport of the time, they regretted that "too often the bicycle is directed not to the church, but past the church". They noted with disappointment that although four-fifths of the younger children attending day school go to Sunday School, attendance lapses as they grow older. The report could have been updated to suit the current situation almost one hundred years later. It was well received by the General Assembly of 1896 and most of the recommendations that it made were implemented by the church over the years; more funds for parochial work, an extension of the ministry by establishing more parishes and more ministers, the appointment of ministers with special responsibilities (the future industrial chaplains) and a closer supervision by presbyteries of the less efficient charges.

*   *   *

For the twenty-seven years the Lang Family were at the Barony, life at 5 Woodlands Terrace was a time of endless activity from early morning till late at night. After they had been in Glasgow for three years the family, now of seven, was complete. By 1876 Patrick, the eldest, was thirteen and David, the youngest, only a few months old, and for about six years the family were all at home, two at the University, four at school and the youngest still a toddler. Grannie Lang was certainly a wonderful person, not only able to manage a family of six lively boys and one girl, but also to take a full part in the work of the parish. And of course without any of the modern means of transport, communication and domestic aids, now all taken for granted. In the latter years of her life when I used to visit her, I remember her as an old lady of great character, living a well-organised life and completely in control of any situation. She had a lovely kind face which so clearly illustrated her nature, and a quiet dry sense of humour which must often have stood her in good stead in managing her family. Understandably Grandfather Lang could spend little time with his family. His was a seven day week but he insisted on spending a few hours of relaxation on a Saturday afternoon with the family making excursions into the country. He was a quick worker and could prepare an important speech in a remarkably short time. He could speak for an hour without a note and he seldom read a speech or a sermon. He would try to spend less time in his study and more time visiting his congregation.

The happiest time of the year was the holiday in the summer when the family left Glasgow bound for the Island of Arran or Speyside, where my grandparents and the family would enjoy picnics and long walks or, for my grandfather and the boys, bathing at the seaside. Then in the evening the family would gather round the lamp and listen to my grandfather reading aloud with dramatic effect the tales of Robert Louis Stevenson and Sir Walter Scott.

6. Principal of Aberdeen University

After twenty-seven years at the Barony, the strain was beginning to tell and my grandfather was looking forward to less arduous work in a country parish. But this was not to be. Quite unexpectedly he received an invitation from Lord Burleigh, the Secretary for Scotland, for his name to be submitted to the Queen for appointment as Vice Chancellor and Principal of Aberdeen University. Now in his sixty-seventh year he had some hesitation in moving to a sphere which would not only be exacting but was a new field of activity for him, but his close friend Lord Strathcona, at that time Rector of the University and later to become its Chancellor, prevailed upon him to accept the position. There was controversy in his appointment which in his disposition he could well have done without. For many years the Principalship had been occupied by a university professor and no doubt there were professors in Aberdeen and in the other Scottish Universities who had their eyes on promotion in this direction. Marshall Lang had had no close connection with university teaching or university administration; he was not an academic and had written little of significance; his career had been in the church and much of his experience in a working class district in Glasgow. But he was known throughout Scotland and held in high esteem as a speaker of distinction, as an able administrator of the church and of his large parish, as a man of wide experience and common sense and notably as one who would move easily into any class of society, even into the more rarified atmosphere of the university common room. After his appointment it was not long before prejudice and opposition were dismissed and by his ability and tact he quickly established himself as an able Principal of the University.

Early in the summer of 1900 my grandparents moved into the Principal's residence, Chanonry Lodge in Old Aberdeen, a charming house only a short distance from King's College and within the precincts of St. Machar's Cathedral, and there they entertained many distinguished visitors who came to the University.

On the business side of the University, when he presided over the University Court in the frequent absence of the Rector, he soon became familiar with the procedures of building and finance and of academic appointments and he took a particular interest in the progress and welfare of the students. On the academic side as chairman of the Senatus he was at first somewhat ill at ease, but by patience and the invaluable advice given him by his close friend and colleague, Mathew Hay, Professor of Medicine, he overcame initial difficulties. On the ceremonial side of the University, he had no equal; his dignity and his eloquence were outstanding.

During his nine years in Aberdeen, there were two notable events, the completion of the Marischal College buildings and the quater-centenary of the University. The extension of the University buildings at Marischal College had been going on for some years before the arrival of my grandfather but it was left to the University Court in his time to complete the magnificent granite frontage of over four hundred feet and the splendid panelled court and faculty rooms within. Difficulties had to be faced; one inevitably was the raising of money, and the other the inclusion into the new frontage of the adjacent church of Greyfriars. To overcome these difficulties, the Principal sought the co-operation of the Lord Provost of Aberdeen, Sir Alexander Lyon, and by the tact of the former and the persistence of the latter, their problems were soon overcome.

The two events were celebrated in circumstances of academic and civic splendour in September, 1906, although the recognition of the quater-centenary of the University had been somewhat belated as King's College was founded in 1495[1]. Some Aberdonians thought that the celebrations were too lavish and that a lesser dignitary than the King might have been invited to open the renovated buildings. But when the time came the people of Aberdeen joined in with great enthusiasm; there was a public holiday, the streets were bedecked with flags and flowers and many insubstantial archways crowned the city streets; fortunately their instability was not tested as the weather throughout was glorious. At his own expense Lord Strathcona had erected a splendid hall for the occasion where he entertained a great gathering from the University and from every walk of city life.

The Principal of course had been heavily involved in all the preliminary arrangements for the celebration and had taken a leading part in all the functions. At the great banquet in Strathcona Hall his oration of welcome to the guests, spoken without a note, was regarded as on of the greatest speeches of his time. In recognition of his distinguished services to his church, the University and his

---

1. There were at one time two separate Universities in Aberdeen. King's College was founded in 1495 and Marischal College in 1593. In 1860 the two colleges were united to become the "University of Aberdeen".

Last days at Chanonry Lodge. The Principal with his wife and family.

country, my grandfather was made a Commander of the Royal Victorian Order in 1906, a month after the memorable celebrations in Aberdeen.

Although now in his seventy-third year, my grandfather had carried out his duties with the vigour of a man in his prime. There was no falter in his rich resonant voice, but the long months of preparation and the responsibilities imposed upon him began to tell upon his strength. His sense of duty and his eagerness spurred him on, although he now seemed to lack some of the zest of earlier years. Towards the end of 1908 he fell ill and his attendance at the University became infrequent. On 2nd May 1909, surrounded by his family, he died at Chanonry Lodge and was buried in the ruined transept of St. Machar's Cathedral, a short distance from the house where he had spent the last nine years of his life. My grandmother moved to a small, secluded house in Ann Street, Edinburgh, where we used to visit her frequently, and there she stayed until she died in 1921.

*   *   *

The life of John Marshall Lang best displays the qualities and traits of his character. In any company my grandfather was immediately recognised by his dignity and his presence and, if he was called upon to speak, he would do so with a clarity and an ease enlivened by a quiet sense of humour. It was said of him that he was a better platform speaker than a preacher, that he could speak to an audience "with a freshness and a vivacity" that was somehow lacking in the pulpit. But even if that was so, he was regarded as one of the most impressive preachers of his day; he had, it was said, "a blessed flow of thought to illustrate the love of God". To those whom he served in his parishes and in the university, he was known for his kindness and his courtesy, but many others whom he met casually could not forget a conversation with this dignified gentleman. On a train journey or in a tram car, he would invariably get into conversation with his neighbours and would almost instinctively share in their worries or their happiness. He was a familiar figure walking in the streets of his parish, and when visiting his people he would be followed by a group of grubby children and often seen holding a sticky hand. When he went to Aberdeen he understood the students of the University perhaps better than any other Principal before him. He would stop them in the street and enquire about their homes and their families, their welfare and their progress, and when discipline was required, he was often regarded as being too lenient. He had seen his own family grow up and had learned from them that mischievous behaviour was seldom malicious. Although in some company he was thought to be reserved, he really loved people, particularly ordinary folk, and it was that bond and that understanding between him and them that made him such a successful parish minister.

He was such an indefatigable worker that apart from his annual holiday he had little time to spend with his family at Morningside and at the Barony. The upbringing of the seven children was left very largely to Grannie Lang, but no doubt there would have been time

The Family of John Marshall Lang 1834-1909 and (m. 1861) Hannah Agnes Keith 1840-1921

| Gavin d. inf. | Patrick Keith 1863-1961 m. Elizabeth Gentle Stevenson | Cosmo Gordon 1864-1945 | Douglas Hamilton 1866-1945 m. Marion Nethersole | Marshall Buchanan 1868-1954 m. Mary Eleanor Farquharson | Hannah Buchanan 1872-1952 m. Robert Barclay | Norman Macleod 1875-1956 m. Monica Crossfield | David Marshall 1876-1925 |

when the family had all gone to bed for the parents to review the events of the day and to iron out any domestic problems that had arisen, and there would certainly have been problems as Patrick and Cosmo were not an easy pair to handle in their youth. My grandfather was a devoted husband and father and was so proud of the success of his children. It was a great disappointment to him that he was unable to attend Cosmo's enthronement as Archbishop of York in 1909 because of the illness which finally caused his death. Grannie Lang writes in the "Memories" of her husband that he had a quick but well-controlled temper, a characteristic which does not seem to have shown itself in his public life, but a characteristic which he certainly handed down to some of his sons.

John Marshall Lang was a true believer and had "a spirit in touch with God". Tributes have been paid to his eloquence, but in his prayers there was a simplicity and a profound sincerity. Every day in the manse there were family prayers and at them my grandfather would pray quietly and earnestly, naming the happenings of the family, for guidance and with gratitude. And in the wider spheres of his parish, his nation and beyond, his prayers in church would be said with equal simplicity and sincerity.

7. The Family of John Marshall Lang
Early Years

As my grandfather moved from parish to parish throughout Scotland so the family were born in different parts of the country. Gavin, Patrick and Cosmo were born in Fyvie, Aberdeenshire; Douglas and Marshall in Glasgow; Hannah in Edinburgh; and finally Norman and David in Glasgow when the family returned there in 1873. Like so many devoted mothers of her time, my grandmother kept a record of the progress of her children in their earliest years, fascinating reading for their descendants more than one hundred years later. Grannie Lang expected too much of her children, she looked for perfection and perhaps fortunately she did not always find it. Whatever they may have become in later life, her family were certainly not saints when they were children.

Gavin, the first-born, was given most attention and seems to have enjoyed perfect health during the four years of his short life, but he had such a restless nature that at the age of three, my grandmother wrote "he would never for two minutes attend to one thing at a time". She regretted his self-will and his impatience but his premature death from whooping cough brought much sorrow to the young parents, who found great solace in their firm faith.

With little more than a year's difference in age, the early characteristics of Patrick and Cosmo were inevitably compared. Cosmo seems to have been a quicker and more intelligent little boy and, according to his mother, would often say, even at this young age, "clever things". But he was not so anxious to be good as Patrick and "hasn't so much reverence or the same strict regard to the truth". Of course in the home there were childish quarrels and fights between the two boys but it seems that "dear Pattie" (as Patrick was called in his early days) frequently got the better of his brother, Cosmo. They progressed in their reading, they sang well and could memorise verses from the Bible. My grandmother records that Patrick got on very well at school and was "always dux of the Bible class". No such success is recorded for the future archbishop who nevertheless is remembered as being "quick and clever at school but very heedless". My grandmother does not hide the fact that both boys could at times be quick tempered, a trait which they may have inherited through the generations from their father, John Marshall, and their grandfather, Gavin. But despite their shortcomings, to my grandmother they were always "very loving affectionate children".

Although Douglas was only two years younger than Cosmo, he did not seem to be a member of the Patrick-Cosmo partnership. He could have stood up to their rough and tumble and given as good as he got, as my grandmother speaks of him as "a sturdy, little fellow, liking his own way". He had less aptitude to learning than his elder brothers but he outshone them in singing although his mother deeply regretted his refusal to learn hymns.

As a loyal son I must quote in full what my grandmother writes about my father: "Marshall is nine months old today. He is the most good natured boy I have ever had, always merry and full of fun". Some years later she speaks well of his speed at learning to read and write and his love of drawing. In later life all the brothers developed a somewhat meticulous talent in drawing and would fill sketch books of country scenes drawn during their holidays. Perhaps because they had more time in later life, Patrick and Douglas painted landscapes in water-colour with great skill. Critics might have said of Douglas that his draughtsmanship was good but that his idea of colour was more imaginative than realistic. A degree of colour blindness has been a weakness of the Lang males for some generations, a fact which may have accounted for Douglas's unusual interpretation of colour.

There were times too when the family would sing together, of sufficient number to form a small harmonious choir with my grandmother, and later her daughter, Hannah, at the piano, It is not known whether they ever gave a public performance but no doubt the Lang choir would be a popular item at any social gathering in the Barony. For two or three years the boys produced a family paper, "The Blackwater Magazine", with Patrick as editor and Cosmo the regular contributor of thrilling tales of adventure. Years later when he was an undergraduate, Cosmo dabbled in journalism and even wrote a novel of which there now seems to be no trace.

The last member of her young family to be mentioned in the records of my grandmother is her only daughter, Hannah of whom she wrote, "My little girl is very engaging — a sweet wee thing, but having impatience of temper".

My grandmother left no record of Norman and David as children. Had there been such a record, it is unlikely that there would have been any mention of "impatience of temper" as they certainly grew up to be the most placid members of her large family.

With a span of only thirteen years between the eldest and the youngest of the seven surviving children, there was a time when all the family were together in 5 Woodlands Terrace. They were brought up within the strict confines of a Victorian household in close comradeship and without extravagance, the means from the stipend of a Church of Scotland minister being very limited. My grandfather, a very busy man, was somewhat aloof from the family leaving the management of the household to my grandmother who was an exceptionally able woman. My uncle Cosmo describes her "in mind and speech as practical, downright, frank and forcible". Her family were devoted to her and regarded her with the greatest respect; certainly to her more than anyone else they attributed their success in later life. She brought them up to be well disciplined and industrious and to value the highest standards of life. To her dying day she showed great interest in all the affairs of her children and grandchildren. In her last letter to my father written in pencil from her bed a few days before she died she wanted to know all about the preparations being made for the wedding of my eldest sister, Hannah.

With such a large family to manage it was necessary to follow a routine. Every morning at the same time the boys would set out for school, and on Sundays, clutching their Bibles and led by their grandmother, they would face the long walk to the Barony Church, only being allowed the luxury of a hansom cab in the stormiest of weather. Many years later an elderly lady who had lived nearby in Woodlands Terrace recalled how in their youth she and her sisters would wait behind the lace curtains of their drawing room window on a Sunday morning to watch "the handsome Lang family" setting off for church and she remembered clearly how on more than one occasion one of the boys would glance a wink in their direction. With hindsight could it have come from my uncle Douglas?

The boys went to the excellent day schools of which there were several in Glasgow, Patrick and Cosmo to Park School under the headmastership of Dr. Collier, a prominent educationalist and historian of his day and an outstanding teacher, and my father, Marshall, first to Albany Academy and later to Glasgow Academy. My uncle Cosmo was a brilliant student; my father, perhaps less so, but he entered wholeheartedly into the life of the school. He was always proud of a team photograph, taken over a hundred years ago with him as a member of the Glasgow Academy Rugby XV, a fine young man with chest extended, arms crossed, proudly wearing the jersey and the tasselled cap of the team.

Patrick, Cosmo and Marshall went on to Glasgow University followed by Norman some years later. Cosmo continued to distinguish himself by carrying off prizes in politics and church history. He was deeply influenced in his youth by the great teachers of his time in Glasgow, especially in philosophy and logic, "They made me think," he wrote many years later, "I almost feel as if I thought more constantly and steadily at sixteen than I have ever done since." In student societies he became an able speaker and debater — woe betide the young man who dared cross words with Cosmo Lang!

Marshall was sixteen when he matriculated as a student at Glasgow University and after seven years he left as a Master of Arts and a Bachelor of Divinity. In his unfinished recollections my father describes his university days as uneventful but a footnote is worth repeating here, "The only political office I have held in my life was that of treasurer of Glasgow University Conservative Club. Many years afterwards I learned from a contemporary student, Bertie Horne, later to become Chancellor of the Exchequer, that my name had been proposed as president of the Club, but that it had been the opinion of the committee that I was 'too damned honest' to hold that office. Instead I became its trustworthy treasurer."

After leaving Glasgow University, the Lang boys went their own ways, grateful throughout their lives that they had had such a sound upbringing. Frequently in later years they recalled the family life in Woodlands Terrace where they all grew up together. Despite the fact, or perhaps because of it, that life was frugal and without any luxury, that discipline was strict and standards of behaviour had at all times to be high, they were happy in their childhood and in their youth; they made their own entertainment and enjoyed the company of one another to such an extent that they seldom made close friendships outside the family circle. Their admiration for their parents was unbounded. Although somewhat austere they recognised their father as a great man with qualities of character and principles they could hardly emulate, but they were closer to their mother who guided their early lives and gave them her understanding and affection.

Although there were common characteristics in this generation of the Lang family, each one mapped out and followed his own career and developed his own personality. Nor must one forget the distinct personality of Hannah, the only daughter in the family. The concluding chapters are devoted to the lives of the six brothers and their sister.

Patrick Keith Lang, the doyen of the family.

8. Patrick Keith Lang, CBE

After the premature death of his brother Gavin (1862-1866), my uncle Patrick — Patrick Keith (1863-1961) became the eldest member of the family of John Marshall and Hannah Lang. Leaving Glasgow University, seemingly before he got his degree, he embarked upon a business career which in its early stages failed to offer him permanent and profitable employment. In less than seventeen years he had moved from Glasgow to India, then to South Africa and finally to Turkey and Egypt, intermittently returning to London for short appointments. With better prospects ahead of him and no doubt through the influence and under the guidance of his uncle, Sir Robert Hamilton Lang, the recently appointed director of the Imperial Ottoman Bank, at the age of thirty-four Patrick joined the bank in Constantinople and seemed destined to follow in the footsteps of his distinguished uncle. Five years later he married Elizabeth Gentle Stevenson of Ingliston (Aunt Bessie) the daughter of a wealthy family with trading interests in Glasgow. Their first home was in Alexandria where the two elder children, Marshall and Elspeth, spent the early years of their lives. Now well established in the Egyptian branch of the Ottoman Bank and on the road to a promising career, an accident happened which changed Uncle Patrick's whole life. He was thrown from his horse in the desert outside Alexandria, suffered severe concussion and before medical help could be got he was given brandy by some well-meaning but misguided Egyptian peasants. From this accident he never fully recovered and for most of his life he endured bouts of extreme head pains, fortunately diminishing as he grew into old age.

The heat and conditions of Egypt were quite unsuitable for his state of health and at the age of forty-one Patrick was obliged to retire from the bank and return with Aunt Bessie and their young family to Britain. For some years they searched Scotland and England for a permanent home suitable for their needs and finally chose to live in Merrow, at that time a charming village on the slopes of the Surrey Downs, a mile or two from Guildford.

The most exciting venture Patrick experienced during these unsettled years was his adoption as Unionist candidate in the 1910 General Election for the Glasgow division of Bridgeton, an area well known to him in his youth when his father was minister of the Barony. For less than three months he nursed his constituency and during the election fought a vigorous campaign supporting Mr. Balfour's policy of tariff reform, of the unity of Great Britain and Ireland, and of the retention of the powers of the House of Lords, and he roundly condemned what he called "the hugger mugger of semi-socialism" of the Liberal government, Not surprisingly in this working class constituency he was unsuccessful, defeated by a Labour opponent, one of 40 members returned at the 1910 election. It was unfortunate for Patrick that his one and only venture into politics at the national level was at a time when the fortunes of the Unionist Party were at a low ebb. He had stood up to the hurly-burly of the election surprisingly well but perhaps not well enough to try again. In any event the opportunity did not arise as the next General Election was not until 1918 when he would probably have been too old to start a political career. Had he been elected in 1910 he would certainly have enjoyed the House of Commons; with his genial disposition he would have made many friends but how successfully his political career would have developed is more doubtful as he lacked that confidence in his own capacity that so often achieves political advancement.

Early in 1915 the family bought Thornechace in Merrow, a beautiful house in its own spacious grounds on the edge of the Downs, but Patrick was to see little of his home until after the war. At the outbreak of war at the age of 51 he was too old for active service, but he threw all his energy into the establishment and organisation of recreation huts behind the lines on the Western Front where war-weary soldiers could enjoy temporary rest and warmth after their ordeals in the trenches. Towards the end of the war he moved to an unpaid post as controller of a department of the Ministry of Reconstruction, finally retiring in 1920 when he was awarded the CBE for his services.

Uncle Patrick (it was about this time that I came to know him) returned to Merrow where he lived the life of a very active country gentleman, becoming a pillar of the community. He rejuvenated the local Men's Club of which he was president for many years, in the summer he bowled on the village green and in the winter acted with the local dramatic society in the village hall; as an ardent conservationist he was keen to maintain the character and beauty of the Merrow Downs, and not surprisingly he was chairman for many years of the Conservative Association, always a profound believer in the value of tradition. He supported the village church, but took little part in its organisation. That sort of thing, he said, he left to his brothers who could do it much better than him. At home he tended his garden with great pride and became an expert topiarist, spending hours clipping his shrubs and hedges with meticulous care and continuing to do so to a great old age within a year or two of his death. His game was tennis which he played with skill and youthful enthusiasm until he was well over seventy. He was fond of travelling and as has already been mentioned he was a water colour painter of some talent.

Uncle Patrick was in his ninety-ninth year when he died in 1961, an age unsurpassed by any member of the Lang family recorded in this history. Aunt Bessie had died eleven years before him and during the infirmity of old age they had been cared for with unsparing devotion by Muriel, the youngest of the family. Throughout the vicissitudes of their early days followed by the more serene years in Merrow, the forty-eight years of their married life had been blissfully happy, a happiness due in no small measure to the patience and understanding of Aunt Bessie. Partly due to the recurring bouts of headache and partly to a natural quickness of temper, characteristic of most of the Langs of his generation, Uncle Patrick could at times be hasty and intolerant but Aunt Bessie understood how to pacify a situation which might lead to family tension. She was such a quiet, kind person who maintained in her life, and handed on to others, the highest standards of Victorian virtues.

Uncle Patrick was known by everyone as being unusually charming and courteous, friendly and approachable but always held in great respect by the local community. He became the doyen of his branch of the Lang family, by far the oldest of his generation, having outlived all his brothers and one sister by several years, He kept in touch with his numerous relatives, taking a great interest in their family affairs. Their frequent visits to Merrow would keep him up to date with the latest family news and were a great joy to him to the end of his long life. He was hospitable and generous. At an early age he had been able to help my father financially to continue his studies in Germany. In a letter dated 1891 my father wrote to Uncle Patrick from Leipzig relating his experiences in Germany and concluding, "And now, old man, I wish I could get hold of your hand and I could give it a right good shake, for whom am I to thank for all this but yourself — a thousand times, nay a thousand times ten thousand . . .". And these act of kindness continued throughtout his life.

He had an impish sense of humour and was a great lover of the practical joke. Those of us who were there will never forget the morning he impersonated Agatha Christie who had mysteriously disappeared from her home not many miles from Merrow and for whom there was a hue and cry around the countryside. One summer morning as we sat at breakfast we watched with astonishment the shadowy figure of a lady wearing a long dress and a large hat flitting around the shrubbery at the bottom of the garden and behaving in a most peculiar manner. Surely this must be the missing Agatha

Christie! Should we approach her and inform the police immediately? Of course it turned out to be Uncle Patrick dressed in Aunt Bessie's clothes. There are other tales of impersonation which have now become legendary in the family.

The serious side of his character was based upon his belief in tradition, but not always convention, He had spent more than half of his life in Surrey in a small Anglican community where the established values of the English public school and Oxbridge were strongly supported and where *The Times* usually, but not always, was the leader of public opinion. But although he was a prominent member of that community he never quite forgot his Presbyterian upbringing, his youth in a Glasgow day school and as a student of Glasgow University and that he spent his early years with people who read the *Glasgow Herald* rather than *The Times*. It was perhaps because of this background and his years in the Middle East that he had a more broad-minded outlook on life than many of his associates in the south of England.

Uncle Patrick died in 1961, greatly beloved and respected by all his relations and friends throughout his long life.

He was survived by his family of three; Marshall who married Margaret Graham in 1935 and died in 1987; Elspeth who married Miles Davies in 1934 and Muriel who remained unmarried.

Cosmo Gordon Lang, the Archbishop.

9. Cosmo Gordon Lang, GCVO, DD, LLD
Oxford, Leeds and Portsea

Cosmo Gordon (1864-1945) — Uncle Cosmo — was undoubtedly the most distinguished of the Langs within the span of this history. For fourteen years he was Archbishop of Canterbury, for many years

more a national figure in church and state, from early years a friend
and associate of kings and throughout his whole life a man of deep
spiritual conviction. But forty years after his death, there is perhaps
little for which he is remembered. The name Cosmo Lang conjures
up to many the part he took in the abdication of Edward VIII, to a
few the coronation of George VI and other royal occasions, and to a
handful an influence in the changing attitude of the religious life of a
nation between two Great Wars. This is not the place for comment or
criticism of these events[1]; our purpose is to relate the events of
Cosmo's life as an important chapter in the family chronicles.

Although he maintained a somewhat distant interest in the family
all his life, he was the first to admit, rather ruefully, that he was not
a good family man. But he was a devoted son, writing regularly and
at length to his mother. She kept all his letters, which have become a
valuable source of biographical material, up to the date of her death
in 1922.

After leaving Glasgow University and going to Oxford, he
became totally dedicated to his profession south of the border,
returning to Scotland only for brief periods during the summer to
enjoy the peace and quiet of his highland home, Ballure in
Argyllshire. Oxford had been the turning point of his life, and
throughout it he cherished his association with the university. When
the occasion was appropriate, he would often repeat his own version
of this relationship.

> "Balliol is my mother, to whom I am bound by ties of
> filial gratitude;
> All Souls is my wife, who gave me a home and most
> generously received me back after a temporary residence
> with
> Magdalen, my very beautiful mistress, for whom
> during three years I forsook my wife!"

It had been a struggle for his parents to send the son of a manse
to Oxford, but his grandmother Keith had come to the rescue and
made it possible, Within a year as an undergraduate at Balliol he had
won the prestigious history prize, the Brackenbury Scholarship, and

---

1 "Cosmo Gordon Lang" by J.C. Lockhard (1949) — the official biography ably
  provides the details of his eventful career.

so the financial strain on the family was lessened. He was sadly disappointed that he only got a "second" in "Greats", but he followed this shortly afterwards by gaining a "first" in Modern History. In other branches of the University, his determination and ambition soon brought this shy, forlorn boy from Scotland into prominence. He summoned up his courage and spoke frequently at the University Union, eventually becoming its President at the age of twenty-one. Such was his reputation as a speaker and debater that at this early age, he was invited to stand for Parliament, but the invitation was refused. Had he accepted and succeeded, his career would have followed a very different line. At the Union, he was the friend and contemporary of young men who were to become prominent in later life, Nathanial Curzon (Viceroy of India and Foreign Secretary), Edward Grey (Foreign Secretary), Huth Jackson (Governor of the Bank of England) and many others. And he too might well have found a place of such distinction.

It had been his intention to become a barrister and with Oxford behind him he would now study for the English Bar and find his way into politics, but the path he followed did not immediately point in that direction. He went to Germany, he interested himself in social work in England, he taught in further education classes and wrote articles for newspapers and magazines, anything to earn a little money as he was almost penniless but was determined to be independent. Meantime his parents in Glasgow were getting impatient. "It's time the boy was starting a career", they would say. But much was forgiven, but perhaps not all, when he was elected a Fellow of All Souls, Oxford, an honour which at least provided him with a roof over his head and a small income for the next seven years; by re-election and honorary appointment he remained a Fellow of All Souls for the rest of his life except for three years when he was a "don" at Magdalen College. At All Souls he was completely relaxed and happy, returning frequently to the peace and quiet of the College as a refuge from the anxieties of his later life.

He was now in a position to complete his legal studies and was shortly to be called to the Bar. Early in 1889 a rare transformation occurred in his life which guided him into the church, to quote his own words "not without heart-searching and pain". For months he had looked for guidance through prayer for a divine calling; he had sought the advice of his close friends, but his parents in Scotland had at first misgivings that the influence of Oxford was leading him towards a Catholicism so contrary to his Presbyterian upbringing. The decision having been taken he would now have to set aside a promising legal career and all the political ambitions he had fostered since his earliest days. He had so many of the qualities required for political success — and he knew it — a sharp and perceptive mind, an impressive speaker, a striking presence and the ambition of a young man who had already made his mark among his political contemporaries. Had his career taken him into politics, there can be little doubt that it would have led him to high office. He would have been a Conservative although he often expressed radical opinions in the House of Lords and he would have competed with, and perhaps surpassed, men of his own age and without great distinction in the Conservative party, such as Bonar Law, Stanley Baldwin and Austen Chamberlain; but how he would have matched the opposition of Lloyd George, with whom he shared almost exactly the same period of life[1] and for whom he had great admiration as a war leader, is more doubtful. He got to know all of them when he was Archbishop and in the House of Lords, and at times he must have pondered as he watched their success that "there but for the grace of God go I".

*   *   *

In preparation for the church, Cosmo studied at Cuddesdon, a college for the training of Anglican priests close to Oxford, and in 1890 he was ordained by the Bishop of Oxford in the local parish church, a place which he often described as "the true Mecca of my religion... the most sacred spot on earth to me". At last he was to tear himself away from Oxford and in complete contrast he became a deacon of the Parish Church of Leeds where for three years he lived and worked with the poorer people of the parish experiencing first-hand, the living conditions and behaviour of the working people of industrial England. On one occasion he was invited to preach at York Minster, a great honour for such a young man, but the Dean of York was embarrassed to find that Cosmo was only a deacon and that it was against the rules for one so lowly to preach in the Minster. When it was learnt that Cosmo was also a Fellow of All Souls, the authorities were satisfied and as such he was admitted to the pulpit of the Cathedral.

During Cosmo's three years at Leeds there had been a closer

---

1. (Lloyd George 1863-1945: Cosmo Lang 1864-1945)

affinity between father and son than any other time in their lives. John Marshall, the father, was now in the mid-term of his ministry in a crowded industrial parish in Glasgow; Cosmo, the son, was now deeply involved in the work of a parish of similar problems in Leeds. His father no doubt had hopes that the mission of his son would continue to be amongst people who were most in need of guidance and support. With his strong Presbyterian tradition, to John Marshall there was no higher calling in the church than that of a parish minister. And it was foremost in Cosmo's mind that he should remain in Leeds for some time. He had now established a reputation, and from various quarters offers came to him which he had seriously to consider for the advancement of his experience and his career. In 1893 he was offered the posts of Dean of Divinity of Magdalen College, Oxford, the Theological Tutor of Balliol College and the Vicar of the Cathedral Church of Newcastle. A Fellowship of Magdalen allowed him residence in the College, the responsibility for teaching in the University and directing the music in Magdalen Chapel, and, as he hastened to remind his father, the pastorate of St. Marys and the duties of a parish minister. All this greatly appealed to Cosmo, so with misgivings he left Leeds and returned to his beloved Oxford.

In his dual capacity at Magdalen and St. Marys, a position unique in the church, every moment of the day was fully occupied, but he rightly felt that he must soon return, however regretfully, to the main stream of church work if he was to advance a career to which he felt he was destined.

His next move was to Portsea as vicar of the sprawling surburban parish of Portsmouth where the men and their families were mainly associated with the navy and the docks. His predecessor had been a hearty muscular Christian who was supported by ten curates of a similar type. Cosmo did not find it congenial to live with and to lead such a rumbustious team. Shortly after his arrival he managed to replace many of the curates by more serious young men from Cuddesdon and Magdalen. The clergy at Portsea lived together in a bachelor house presided over by the vicar who ruled the monastic establishment with a rod of iron. He found the management and leadership in an active working class parish an essential part of his own training and experience, often recalling later in his York and Canterbury days the hard work and long hours he devoted to his parishioners in Portsea.

By contrast it was while he was at Portsea that Cosmo was given an introduction to royal circles which influenced him throughout the rest of his life. Osborne, on the Isle of Wight, where Queen Victoria spent most of the last years of her long life, was near Portsea and news had reached the old Queen that the vicar of Portsea was an excellent preacher and a promising young man in the Church. He was invited to preach in the royal chapel and to stay at Osborne, making such an impression on the Queen that his visits continued frequently for the rest of her life. She enjoyed his sermons and was able to compare them with one she had heard from his father at Balmoral; but more than that she enjoyed talking to him and confiding in him some of the affairs of state. She advised him to marry and suggested to him that a wife would be more of a help to him than all his curates. "No doubt, ma'am", he replied", "but there is a difference: if a curate proves to be unsatisfactory I can get rid of him. A wife is a fixture." As a chaplain to Her Majesty, he assisted at her funeral in 1901, the first of a series of royal occasions when Cosmo was to take a prominent part in the ceremonies.

10. <u>C.G.L.</u> — <u>Stepney and York</u>

Five years at Portsea and then another step in the ladder of his distinguished career, this time to become Bishop of Stepney and Canon of St. Pauls. At the age of 37, for the first time he set up his own house with his own staff in 2 Amen Court, under the shadow of St. Paul's Cathedral. Although now a suffragan bishop he continued to live the spartan life he had become accustomed to in earlier years. The furnishings of Amen Court were simple, he slept on an iron bedstead and the food he ate was frugal, even when he entertained visitors. This was the pattern throughout his life. Although at Bishopthorpe and Lambeth when he became Archbishop there was an outward show of grandeur with butlers and footmen, his own living quarters were plain, to say the least. He seemed to enjoy the contrast of the grand life which inevitably he followed as an Archbishop with the simple living which he chose for himself.

In his association with people it was the same. The diocese of Stepney included some of the poorest parts of London; Whitechapel, Hackney, Bethnal Green to mention a few; but although he was a bishop, he did not distance himself from the everyday problems of his people. He assisted in the improvement of working conditions and housing within the diocese, he visited boys' clubs, workhouses and the homes of the poor and elderly and would discuss the social affairs of the diocese with the social reformers of this day who seemed to collect around Stepney; Beatrice and Sidney Webb, Keir Hardie, George Lansbury and perhaps even the young Clement Attlee at Toynbee Hall.

During his seven years at Amen Court he was a very busy man. In addition to the endless programme of pastoral work, he took a full part in the life of St. Paul's, frequently preaching in the great cathedral and, having such a reputation as a preacher, being constantly in demand to address meetings and conduct services outside the diocese. Added to all this, more and more he became the assistant to the Bishop of London, the ageing Dr. Ingram who increasingly relied upon the help and advice of the young Bishop of Stepney.

*   *   *

In 1909 Uncle Cosmo (by this time I was his nephew) at the age of forty-four became Archbishop of York, as some said later in his life "too young for York and too old for Canterbury" to which See he was translated twenty years later. The move from Stepney to York was to change his life; he quickly became a national figure, he assumed far greater responsibilities in church and state, and he enjoyed his place in Yorkshire society as the squire of Bishopthorpe, the ancient and spacious residence of the archbishop, a beautiful house three miles from the City of York on the banks of the River Ouse. His predecessor, Dr. Maclagan, who had retired at the age of eighty-two, had in his latter years allowed the residence and the garden to become neglected. Uncle Cosmo immediately improved the property. The house was refurnished, but the iron bedstead remained for some years until a friend secretly replaced it by a more comfortable bed, a change which the archbishop regretted as he said it removed "his last link with the Apostles". Although he had not previously been particularly interested in gardens, the garden at Bishopthorpe became his pride and joy, a showpiece in the north of England with a beautiful herbaceous border. He would delight in escorting his many visitors round the garden and to their surprise would identify all the species of flowers. He was able to continue this interest until the last days of his life, as King's Cottage where he lived after retirement had a private door to Kew Gardens. Wandering round the gardens in his old age gave him great pleasure, enjoying their beauty and their interest without having any responsibility for their upkeep.

There were frequent visitors to Bishopthorpe, many of them official and coming from the 659 parishes of his diocese; others from his wide circle of friends would stay longer, but one who regularly spent Christmas with him was his mother. She had attended his enthronement at York Minster but because of ill health and to his great sorrow his father who died a few months later had not been able to travel the long journey from Aberdeen. With his closest friends, often from Oxford days and usually from outside the circle of the Church, Uncle Cosmo was a genial host, but many of the clergy of his diocese and their wives found a visit to Bishopthorpe something of an ordeal. It was difficult for them to change the formality of the occasion and any attempt to break the ice by some familiarity on their part would quickly be stifled by the Archbishop. His manner did not help people who were seemingly overawed by him, yet he liked company and particularly the company of women

The Archbishop and his mother.

who could "sparkle" — his own word — in his presence. Once the barrier was broken he would respond and would warmly appreciate their company. The elderly Dr. Gore, the Bishop of Oxford, is quoted as saying, "Lang would be a dear delightful boy if he were not so terribly archiepiscopal".

The resident chaplains of the Archbishop were carefully chosen, often from among the clergy he had known in earlier years. It was certainly not an easy assignment. In the performance of their duties Uncle Cosmo would expect perfection. There was no excuse if anything went wrong. Like his brothers he could be impatient and often intolerant, but at the same time he would be the first to praise a job well done. Once I had occasion when he was at Lambeth to call at the Palace and enquire about his health when he was ill and was told by his chaplain, "When I tell you your uncle's temper is a little better to-day, you may be reassured he is on the mend."

Stafford Crawley, for many years a chaplain at Bishopthorpe, became one of his closest friends and it was the Crawley family who gave to Uncle Cosmo something he had lacked since the days of Woodlands Terrace — a taste of family life. Previously all his chaplains had been bachelors. Stafford Crawley and his family lived under the same roof occupying the west wing of Bishopthorpe and Uncle Cosmo loved having the family around him. There were horses in the stables, he made two tennis courts for them in the grounds and no party at Christmas or on birthdays was complete without the Archbishop. Their presence was really a godsend to Uncle Cosmo at a particularly difficult period in his life.

He continued to be a tireless worker, administering the affairs of the diocese and visiting as often as he could the parishes within its bounds. There had to be frequent visits to London to confer with his Archbishop colleague of Canterbury and he seldom missed an important debate in the House of Lords, often speaking on social and economic matters. His maiden speech aroused the criticism of his right wing friends when he supported Lloyd George's "People's Budget", recalling as he spoke the deprivation he had seen in Stepney and Leeds. In the House of Lords where quiet and reasoned argument was expected he had few rivals in his day. Like his father he was a first class after-dinner speaker with an apt turn of phrase and a ready wit and if a great gathering had to be addressed he could leave his audience spellbound. On the many national occasions when he was called upon to preach as Archbishop, he was able usually to reflect the feelings of the nation.

The years of the 1914-18 war was a period of great anxiety for him and was shown in the change of his appearance. He had gone to York in 1909 a man upright and young for his years; ten years later he had developed a stoop and had lost all his thick black hair and become a venerable old man. Almost every family in his diocese had suffered bereavement and many of his clergy who had volunteered for service never returned, often leaving widows and families in straitened circumstances. He visited the Western Front and the fleet and was asked by the government to go to America to plead the allied cause. On one occasion because of an inept reference in a speech to the Kaiser which the press and public were not ready to forgive, he aroused war hysteria against himself, an incident which hurt him very deeply.

11. C.G.L. — Canterbury

In 1928 at the age of sixty-four Uncle Cosmo became Archbishop of Canterbury, sadly leaving the companionship of the Crawley family and his beautiful house and garden at Bishopthorpe, his home for twenty years. Lambeth Palace in the heart of London was less of a home to him than a headquarters of the Church of England. For him there was no respite from the constant visits of Anglican clergy from all quarters of the globe. Hospitality was nearly always official and visitors resident in the Palace were invariably there for a purpose rather than for pleasure. As often as he could he would escape — perhaps only to be faced with further duties — to the Old Palace at Canterbury, a quiet and beautiful residence beside the Cathedral.

Shortly after his enthronement, Uncle Cosmo suffered the first serious illness of his life and was obliged to give up his duties for several weeks. His impatience to deal with his mounting correspondence and the problems that beset him did not help his recovery. Naturally as a new archbishop, he had plans he wanted to initiate and there were matters he could not easily delegate, but for a time these had to be set aside. His chaplains knew only too well that delegation had never been his practice. They had frequently urged him to leave the less important matters to them but in vain. He returned to his onerous tasks too soon and within two years he had another serious illness from which he took longer to recover. It was more than three years after his enthronement at Canterbury that he was restored to health but those who knew him thought that some of the vitality of earlier years had gone.

In his sermon at his enthronement the new Archbishop made a plea for unity within the Church of England and for a closer relationship with other churches. But there was little time to achieve his aims. For his first three years as Archbishop he had been handicapped by ill health and during his last three years the nation was at war. In the intervening period he found that the machinery of the Church, like the mills of God, ground so slowly that he was exasperated by the lack of progress in fulfilling his aims. He presided with great skill over the Lambeth Conference as he did over so many other great church gatherings and innumerable church committees but the compromise decisions that frequently had to be reached were often not to his liking and indecision and procastination irritated him. In his efforts to promote closer understanding with other churches, progress was invariably hampered by the inability of churches, not least his own, to move from entrenched positions. With the church of his forbears, the Church of Scotland, he found that a closer communion with Presbyterianism was not to be achieved in his lifetime. The rejection by Parliament of his proposals to revise the Prayer Book, something for which he had worked so hard for so long, was a sore disappointment to him. And added to all this, there was the day to day work of the church at home and abroad, with so many personal matters affecting the clergy and their families which were often more worrying to him than the greater issues. "Clergy are very troublesome people" he once wrote to his chaplain.

His attendances at the House of Lords which he had enjoyed in his earlier days were now less frequent and limited to occasions when he had to speak. As an elder statesman he was invited to become a member of Royal Commissions on Education and on the Indian Constitution. His part in the abdication of Edward VIII in 1936 greatly distressed him as his friendship with the Royal Family had been close for many years and he had formed an admiration and affection for Edward when he was Prince of Wales. In a broadcast after the abdication he roundly condemned the behaviour of the social world with whom the ex-king had been closely associated and was denounced for doing so by the supporters of that society. But he was only saying what a great many people felt ought to be said.

*   *   *

May 12th 1937 was described by Uncle Cosmo as the culminating day of his official life when King George VI and Queen Elizabeth were crowned by him in Westminster Abbey. Preparation for this great occasion of drama and pageantry had been started months before and had been done with such meticulous care by the Archbishop and the young Earl Marshal, the Duke of Norfolk, that the great ceremony passed without a hitch. Uncle Cosmo afterwards confessed that he had enjoyed every moment of it. At the age of seventy-three it had not taxed his strength unduly, the many tributes of praise from all over the world being a great encouragement to him. The ceremony had been broadcast and filmed and millions had appreciated the faultless performance of the Archbishop.

At the same time Uncle Cosmo took the opportunity of presenting to the nation the religious significance of the ceremony and of seeking a reaffirmation of the spiritual life of the people. It was undoubtedly a disappointment to him that his "Recall to Religion" had made little or no impact on the millions who had enjoyed the drama of the Coronation and the parties that followed. He blamed himself for his failure to make a more lasting impression upon the people of the country.

*   *   *

After fourteen years as Archbishop of Canterbury, Uncle Cosmo resigned at the end of March 1942. He was in his seventy-eighth year and it was the view of many at that time that he had held on too long, particularly as the church was looking for younger leadership during the dark days of the war. He probably should have made the decision to resign after the Coronation in 1937, as indeed he was encouraged to do by his chaplains and others to whom it was apparent that the pressure of work was telling upon him. During the war, life was very difficult for the ageing Archbishop. His residence in London became a fortified Lambeth Palace, the garden was a collecting point for barrage balloons,[1] one of the towers of the palace was an RAF observation post and the crypt, a shelter for 200 people. The palace was bombed three times while he was Archbishop, once when he was resident and had a very narrow escape.

Extracts from letters to my father during the war years relate some of the experiences my uncle had to face at that time.

Lambeth Palace 12.9.40

". . . I am glad to hear that though you have the usual visit of bombs they have not come very near your home. I wish I could say this either of Lambeth or of Canterbury. The nights at Lambeth are a great trial. All night long the droning of these enemy bombers and the sound of crashing bombs so loud that they seem sometimes to be actually on

---

1. In "Downing Street Diaries, 1939-1955" (p.44), John Colville, at that time Private Secretary to the Prime Minister, writes:

   In the morning I walked to Lambeth Palace to discuss Ecclesiastical matters with the Archbishop of Canterbury. He was very charming and patriarchal . . . and every now and then introduced a sly sense of humour into his conversation which was most disarming. "That", he said, pointing to a barrage-balloon in the garden, "they call the Arch-blimp!"

the house. Last night, however, we had a welcome relief when most of the noise came from our own anti-aircraft guns which bespattered the enemy with shells and kept him at bay. At Canterbury last afternoon, a terrific bomb crashed within 30 yards of the old Palace and smashed the lovely house of my former chaplain, Sargent, now Archdeacon of Maidstone. It is marvellous that the Cathedral escaped. I spend my time between Lambeth and Canterbury and though there are dangers at Canterbury yet the noise is less incessant than here at Lambeth . . ."

Lambeth Palace 26.9.40 (Dr. Don, chaplain to the Archbishop, to my father).

". . . The Archbishop is spending most of his time at Canterbury and it is just as well, because early on Friday morning Lambeth Palace was hit by a couple of bombs which exploded in the drawing room and reduced that part of the house to ruins. Had the Archbishop been in residence he would have escaped with the skin of his teeth. The blast expended itself against the wall of his bedroom and did not do any serious damage to his suite of rooms. It is a sad ending to his Archiepiscopate, for there is no chance of Lambeth Palace being restored to normal use until after the war — if then! . . ."

Old Palace, Canterbury 4.10.40

". . . It is of course very sad for me to reflect that in all probability I shall not be able to live again in a house which has meant so much to me as well as to the whole Church of England. I must make my headquarters at this house at Canterbury though even here we are far from safe. When we have to go up to London I must live in the Lorrards Tower, which is attached to the Palace as you know and which, I suppose, is as safe as any other place there . . ."

Old Palace, Canterbury 28.3.41

". . . You are right in thinking that I am in very good health though it is awkward to be living mainly here and only going up to Lambeth very occasionally during the week as I can no longer live there, and all this talk about the possibility of invasion makes my continued residence even here very doubtful as I shall not be permitted to decide for myself . . ."

The conclusion of this letter is an oblique reference to a warning by the military authorities that should the Germans invade the south-east of England, it was known that the kidnapping of the Archbishop would be a valuable prize for the enemy.

Despite everything, he faced all these difficulties with equanimity and was determined to continue his duties as far as he was able, visiting throughout his diocese and travelling up to London by means of transport he had never previously experienced, once on a coal lorry when his car had broken down. To resign at such a time would, he felt, be to abdicate his duties. Encouraged by the King, but not by the Prime Minister, the decision was taken and after 52 years of service to the church and the nation, he resigned.

Resignation brought personal problems. He had no house, few savings and only a small pension, but his friends came to the rescue. An anonymous beneficiary helped him financially and the King gave him the life use of a charming residence, King's Cottage, adjoining Kew Gardens. There he lived quietly and happily in good health for the remaining three years of his life enjoying the beauty of the gardens, still attending the House of Lords (he had been made a baron, Lord Lang of Lambeth, on retirement) and engaging himself in church affairs until the day of his death. He died suddenly, waiting for a bus, on 5th December, 1945.

Three of the four surviving members of the family of eight attended the funeral of my uncle at Westminster Abbey. My father, recovering from an illness, was unable to join them but his brothers and sister wrote to him giving their own accounts of the funeral services.

Uncle Patrick, then in his 83rd year, wrote:

". . . Well, well. It is all over. The Service at the Abbey was most impressive but I had the illusion of seeing Cosmo Ebor and Cosmo Cantuar figuring at the long procession of dignitaries as in former solemn occasions and it was beyond me to believe that his dignity was encased on the be-candelled bier. The family were together near the catafalque — . . . — but only Norman, Hannah and I followed the coffin the length of the Abbey, I with

Hannah, Norman following. And he was Normanic
wearing his rain coat and skull cap! Hannah and I
witnessed the placing the coffin in the hearse that was to
proceed to Canterbury. Norman had disappeared in search
of his umbrella about which he was agitated as it was
pre-war. (It had been retrieved by Elspeth!). Norman was
to accompany the cortege to Canterbury and I am glad of
that . . ."

Uncle Norman described the service at Canterbury, conducted
before cremation and the depositing of the ashes in the St. Stephen's
Chapel of the Cathedral.

". . . The Canterbury service was similar to
Westminster in form, but much more moving. It was his
home and his own Cathedral which he loved, filled from
end to end with his own clergy and people. Westminster
was national: but Canterbury was pastoral and personal. It
was very beautiful, in setting and music, and rendering and
simple sincerity . . ."

Aunt Hannah attended a memorial service at St. Paul's
Cathedral a few days later and wrote:

". . . You will want to have a brief account of the St.
Paul's service to-day. There was this appeal about it for
me personally that there was none of the fuss and bother
of Westminster about seating and of course there was the
quiet and help of the Holy Communion. But, my dear —
chilly physically and spiritually. It didn't seem to me as if
there were any, or only a few of his own personal friends
among the dignitaries — as if they were there as part of
their job. As for the Bishop of London — he seemed to be
put in the pulpit — to read an address! I only heard a
word here and there and I was well to the front. What I
did hear was unconvincing and his delivery more so. I only
hope other people were differently affected. The nave was
full almost to the back and there was a goodly array of
dignataries . . ."

12. C.G.L. The Archbishop and the Family Man

After his mother's death in 1922, Uncle Cosmo's contacts with his relations north of the border were intermittent. There were occasional visits by members of our family to Bishopthorpe and Lambeth and one to King's Cottage at Kew, and in return he came to stay with us occasionally at the manse at Whittingehame, our home for many years, on his way north to Ballure on the west coast of Scotland. He called his annual pilgrimage to the north "the Snob's Progress" as he travelled from one great house to another. Since becoming Archbishop he had developed a propensity for the aristocracy and the noble families of "Burke's Peerage", a marked contrast to the style of life he had lived so closely with the working people of Leeds, Portsea and London in the early years of his career. A visit to Whittingehame Manse brought him back to reality. As he sat at the mid-day dinner table with the family of his brother Marshall, and with my mother cooking and serving the meal, he must have been reminded of his own upbringing in Woodlands Terrace, Glasgow. He would never spend more than two nights at Whittingehame and then it would be on to Balmoral to stay with the King and Queen.

My uncle was a good correspondent, writing briefly and to the point by return of post to letters from my father who had usually written to him commenting on some event in his career. In his reply any mention of matters of church and state would be terse, concluding with a short enquiry about family affairs and an expression of brotherly affection. Fortunately most of Uncle Cosmo's letters were typed as his handwriting was often almost indecipherable. Two letters are worth recording in a family history.

The first (in his own handwriting) to my father after he had been invited to preach for his first time at Crathie, the church attended by the Royal Family when at Balmoral.

Balmoral Castle
Sept, 6, 1912

My dear Marshall,
The King has told me that you are to preach here during his residence. I congratulate you very heartily on

this honour. It is not my doing: I suppose Sibbald[1] suggested it: but the King said he wanted to hear my minister brother. I fear you may be rather "put out" by this honour: but I write to pass on some of my long experience that the less you bother about it the better. There are two golden rules for these occasions, (1) Be brief (2) Be simple. As to (1) I know the King (is limited in) his taste! fidgets after quarter of an hour — aim at that time.

About (2) don't think you are addressing Kings and such like at all. Speak as if you were addressing an ordinary congregation of fair intelligence. The less elaborate you are the better. If you can speak rather than read your sermon, it will make it the more appreciated but do just as you are accustomed to do anywhere else.

If you dine in the evening, Sibbald will tell you all that is required in the way of dress and etiquette. Bow slightly when you shake hands with the King and Queen, address them as "Sir" or "Ma'am" with an occasional "Your Majesty" thrown in, not too elaborately: and remember they are ordinary human beings: and everybody wants to be kind. So good luck to you!

Yrs. aff.

Cosmo Ebor

The second letter was written from Bognor where Uncle Cosmo was recovering from his illness after his appointment to Canterbury. The house which he occupied happened to be next to the house where King George V was also convalescing after a serious illness. As old friends they were able to meet frequently and Uncle Cosmo wrote to my father on 20th March 1929.

". . . You may be interested to hear that last week I had a long talk with the King, the first of his subjects outside his family and immediate household to see him and I was amazed and greatly pleased at finding him so much himself and able to talk brightly and fully. I was pleased that he allowed to dwell on some of the deeper aspects of

1. Minister of Crathie

his long trial. I am lunching with the Queen to-day and I
hope that the first official function of the King after his
recovery will be to receive the Homage of the two
Archbishops . . ."

It was on one of these visits that Uncle Cosmo found the King
on the beach at Bognor building sandcastles with his grand-daughter,
the future Queen Elizabeth; a delightful picture of two monarchs
building sandcastles to be blessed by an Archbishop!

Throughout his long ministry Uncle Cosmo had been close to the
Royal Family and had known six monarchs during his lifetime. As
vicar of Portsea he had frequently visited Queen Victoria at Osborne.
Not surprisingly his relationship with Edward VII was less familiar
although it was Edward who had stamped the seal of his appointment
to the archbishopric of York. He rightly claimed to be a close friend
of George V. They were the same age having been born within a few
months of one another, and throughout his reign Uncle Cosmo was
his Archbishop at York and Canterbury, assisting in the coronation of
the King, preaching at his great Jubilee service at St. Pauls and
finally conducting his funeral service at Windsor. They met frequently
in London, but it was during his annual visits to Balmoral where
there was less formality that the King and the Archbishop formed a
firm friendship.

They did not always agree. Kenneth Rose in his biography of
King George V tells a story of how on one occasion they were at
odds.

"Not every preacher to the King came through the
ordeal with credit. There was an early brush with Cosmo
Lang. Against the King's known wishes, he took as his
theme Christian missions overseas, an endeavour which the
King thought both intrusive and futile. At lunch afterwards
they had a set to. Lang told the King that being a
Christian carried with it belief in the world wide mission of
Christianity. 'Then you tell me that with my views that I
cannot be a Christian?, the King asked. Lang replied that
he could only state the premises, it was for the King to
draw the conclusions. 'Well, I call that damned cheek',
said the King."

At Balmoral the Archbishop frequently accompanied the Queen

on her afternoon drives around Deeside while the King spent much of his time shooting on the moors. He found the Queen intellectually more intelligent than her husband; they would talk together about books and gardens, travel, and of course antique furniture, an interest which the Archbishop shared with the Queen. With the King the conversation would be confined to contemporary political personalities and the current affairs of state; on other matters such as shooting and stamps Uncle Cosmo had no views.

A story is told when one day the Archbishop was invited to walk the hills with the shooting party. While he waited for the guns to finish their drive, he rested on a rock and fell fast asleep. When he awoke he discovered to his dismay and fear that a golden eagle was hovering overhead. "No doubt", said the King when he heard of the Archbishop's plight, "you felt that you were mounting up as wings with eagles." To which the Archbishop replied, "The text which came to my mind was 'Wheresoever the carcase is, there will the eagles be gathered together.'"

Uncle Cosmo paid his last visit to Balmoral in the summer of 1935. In January of the following year the King died at Sandringham with the Queen and the Archbishop at his bedside. The week that followed and the royal funeral in London and Windsor were days of great emotional strain for the Archbishop; for him it was more than a royal event of national mourning, it was a time of personal sorrow with the passing of a close friend.

As Archbishop of Canterbury he was of course deeply involved in the abdication of King Edward VIII and the following year with great pageantry he crowned King George VI and Queen Elizabeth at Westminster Abbey. His friendship with the Royal Family was renewed with this younger generation and he often expressed his gratitude to the young monarch for his kindness in granting to him the life occupancy of "the grace and favour" property of King's Cottage on Kew Green.

*   *   *

Although he had spent all his career in England, Uncle Cosmo never forgot that he was a Scot with a great love of Scotland, particularly the Scottish Highlands. He treasured the memories of his Scottish upbringing and of his deep affection for his mother. The happiest month of his year was spent in Scotland in the simplicity of his beautiful home at Ballure, Argyllshire, where he would tramp the hills, often with his brother, Norman, or with a few of his privileged friends. This was also the time to recharge his spiritual batteries by spending hours in contemplation and prayer in a little chapel annexed to his house, which he called his "Cell".

In his youth he had been brought up in the Church of Scotland and no doubt he had been admitted by his father as a communicant of that Church. But Oxford and Cuddesdon had converted him and established his belief in episcopacy. It was always his intention to work increasingly to promote the unity of the church in the United Kingdom but so firmly did he hold to the tenets of Episcopacy that for him any ecumenical advance with Presbyterianism could go so far but no further, the barrier being any participation in the sacraments of the Anglican communion by those not ordained in Episcopacy. When my father was Moderator of the Chuch of Scotland, he visited the Sudan, and was invited by the Bishop of the Sudan, the saintly Bishop Gwynne, to assist him in the Anglican communion service in Khartoum Cathedral. When it came to his notice that a Presbyterian minister, albeit his brother, had assisted in the celebration of an Anglican communion service, the Archbishop was furious and wrote a stern rebuke to the Bishop. To his brother, he wrote coldly, "I make no comment on the Bishop's invitation to you at that Celebration of the Holy Communion". On other matters, Uncle Cosmo was enthusiastic in his praise that there had been such a close and happy relationship between the Anglican Cathedral in the Sudan and the Church of Scotland. But for him Bishop Gwynne had on one occasion gone beyond the precepts of the Church.

* * *

The last years of Uncle Cosmo's life were happier than he had expected. He was afraid that as he would no longer be the centre of the stage, life would become uneventful and uninteresting. But he found he had plenty to occupy his mind; he still attended the House of Lords and spoke infrequently, he was a trustee of the British Museum and in addition to other matters there was always the attraction of the neighbouring Kew Gardens where he assumed almost a proprietary interest, becoming friendly with many of the gardeners. Without the almost intolerable burden of responsibility, work and correspondence, he was more relaxed and displayed a side of his nature seldom seen during his busy life. Like other great public figures, there was more than one side to his character. As Archbishop he had all the qualities which brought him to the summit of his profession; intellect and industry, ability, integrity and dignity, ambition and above all a deep spirituality, but it was another side of his character that showed his humanity. He never forgot the beginnings of his career as a priest with a real zeal for work among under-privileged people, but although his public performances in his later years may seem to have overshadowed his early concern, he was always mindful of the experiences during his ministry in Leeds, Portsea and London.

Was it true, as he said of himself, that he was not a good family man? He valued his upbringing as a boy in Glasgow: he had the greatest respect for his father and a deep affection and regard for his mother from whom who he inherited many of his finest qualities. He certainly had a great interest in and concern for their welfare. As a bachelor — and he was so not because of any belief in the celibacy of the priesthood — he lacked that closer contact with his brothers and sister and their families that a wife would have brought. There was no hint in his correspondence or conversation that he seriously contemplated matrimony at any time. Although he had qualities that must have attracted many admirers, throughout his whole life he was so fully dedicated to his work that he had no time to follow the advice Queen Victoria had given him. Nor indeed in his early years had he the means to support a wife in the style that he himself would have wished, In writing to my father he showed concern for the family by usually concluding his letter with some reference to a family matter, indicating that he had perhaps more interest in their affairs than we had ever imagined.

As a family we were proud of his success and would follow with the greatest interest the events of his illustrious career. There were certainly many sides to his character. Sir William Orpen, who found great difficulty in painting his portrait, said, "I see seven Archbishops. Which am I to paint?" One of his contemporaries spoke of him as "proud, prelatical and pompous". His friend and mentor, Bishop Gore, described him as always being "terribly archiepiscopal". But to our generation of the family he was "Uncle Cosmo", to meet at first sometimes a little austere as if his thoughts were elsewhere, but within a moment and with that twinkle in his eye and that smile on his lips, he would become the family man, enquiring, discussing and advising about family affairs as if little else mattered.

13. Douglas Hamilton Lang

After leaving school, Douglas Hamilton Lang (1866-1945) — Uncle Douglas — did his apprenticeship as a chartered accountant in Glasgow before going to South Africa at the age of twenty-three. He used to joke that his first job in South Africa was that of a barman; whether this is true or not has never been established. Throughout his life many of his stories, famous or infamous, had to be taken with a pinch of salt as he shared that Lang characteristic of being able to make a good tale from a grain of truth. Little is known of his early years in South Africa or why he went there at all. If the story is true, that he was once a barman, perhaps only occasionally to supplement his meagre income, he would have done the job well as he had qualities of cheerfulness and friendliness which were always part of his character.

Hard work in his profession as an accountant brought its reward. By 1897 he had become secretary of the Rand Mines Group in Johannesburg. It was then that he met Clive Parker (my father-in-law), an engineer in the group, who introduced him to Marion Nethersole, Clive's sister-in-law, (Aunt Minnie). After a brief courtship they married in 1898 when Douglas was thirty-two years of age. They made their home in the Transvaal where they continued to live for over thirty years, taking an active part in the affairs of the growing community. Uncle Douglas interested himself in the Anglican Church of the new mining town of Roedepovrt where he carved a wooden altar, still used to this day, a memorial to his dedication to the church.

After seven years with the Rand Mines Group, he started in practice on his own as a chartered accountant and built up a very successful business. So highly was he thought of in his professional work that he was appointed Registrar of Accountants and later played an active role in forming the Chartered Accountants Society of South Africa.

After he retired at the age of 64, he and Aunt Minnie spent several years in England renewing the acquaintance of the relatives and friends they had not seen for many years. In fact they seriously thought of settling in England, but the call of their family and the warmth of the climate they missed so much made the decision easier for them to return to the Cape Province in South Africa. Aunt Minnie died in 1940 and Uncle Douglas in 1945. They had two daughters, Grace who died at the age of eleven, and Monica who married Edward Buchanan, a partner of Uncle Douglas. She died in the early 1970s.

Uncle Douglas had many of the characteristics of his brothers, their stature and their handsome features and a fine clear voice with only the trace of a South African accent although he had lived in that country for so long. He shared the charm and courtesy of his generation and had a sense of humour which could at times be mischievous. But like his brothers he inherited the family failing of occasional intolerance and quick temper. Professionally in the business world of South Africa he had been successful. He had gone there without prospects or influence and thirty years later when he retired he was recognised as one of the most respected accountants in the country.

As one who had lived so long overseas, he had naturally a broader outlook on life than his brothers and sister who came to accept, or ignore, his occasional unconventional behaviour. There were times when he would mildly scorn the life of "the establishment" in which they lived. On one occasion at a Lambeth Palace reception to which he had been invited, he chatted to a group of dignitaries in a broad Glasgow accent relating to them how he and his brother, the Archbishop, had spent their youth in Glasgow. The Archbishop was not amused.

Uncle Douglas was certainly "a character", often a trial to his long suffering wife, Aunt Minnie, but to us, the younger members of the family, he was always great fun, an amiable and very friendly person. It is not without reason that he was known as "the joker of the pack".

14. Marshall Buchanan Lang, TD, DD
Early Years, Old Meldrum and Dundee

Marshall Buchanan Lang, the Moderator.

My father — Marshall Buchanan Lang (1868-1954) was the only member of the family to follow in the footsteps of his father and grandfather into the ministry of the Church of Scotland. As a student at Glasgow University he had the opportunity to assist his father in many of the activities of the Barony Church and as a divinity fledgling he had been encouraged to conduct services in the missions of the parish. Not yet licensed to preach he was not admitted to the pulpit of the Barony, a privilege which he later enjoyed with pride when he became fully ordained.

After graduation in 1890 through the generosity of his elder brother Patrick, he was able to go to the German University of Göttingen where he continued his study of theology and philosophy and fraternised happily with his German colleagues. There followed a short course of study at Leipsig University before he returned to Scotland to be "licensed" (a term to which he strongly objected) to preach by the Presbytery of Glasgow.

An essential part of the training of a minister of the Church of Scotland is serving as an assistant to a senior minister. My father was particularly fortunate in his assignments, serving under three ministers with great distinction at that time. The first was Dr. John Macleod, minister of Govan Parish Church, one of the stalwarts of the ministry, "as stalwart in form and figure as he was in faith". Having learnt much from Dr. Macleod for nearly two years, it was suggested that he should accept the offer of another assistantship at Kinnoull, near Perth, with Dr. Anderson who, it was thought, was likely to demit his office owing to age and infirmity and that his assistant, if he appeared worthy, might have a reasonable chance of succession. Although over 80 years of age, the old man made a wonderful recovery after an operation, and to the delight of his parishioners he was able to resume his work for several more years.

So my father moved to his third term of probation, now with Dr. George Matheson of St. Bernard's Church, Edinburgh, a position which proved to be of great importance in his life and in his career. Mary Eleanor Farquharson was a young and very lively member of the St. Bernard's congregation. Through the activities of the church, she and my father met frequently and to no one's surprise they fell in love and were married shortly after my father's appointment to his first parish of Old Meldrum, Aberdeenshire. Theirs was a marriage of great happiness and devotion which lasted almost 57 years to the day. The important part my mother played in the family history is written in a later chapter.

Dr. George Matheson was a truly remarkable man. Totally blind from his youth, he had the courage to undertake the onerous work of a busy city parish; he was a poet, a composer of hymns, and a forthright and commanding preacher delivering his sermons in a rich Scottish accent; my father recalls him as a very lovable character with a keen sense of humour. My father had endless stories about his association with Dr. Matheson. Being blind, the Doctor would commit his carefully prepared sermons to memory and would seldom falter in the pulpit. But there was one dreadful hour when memory failed and there followed an embarrassingly long pause in his oratory. Seemingly he glowered at his congregation. "My memory's gone", he declared, "and you can go, too". Hurriedly pronouncing the benediction, he dismissed the congregation.

On another occasion a divinity professor had been invited to preach at St. Bernard's. His sermon had already long outlasted the recognised time when to the relief of the congregation he reached the point, as most sermons do, when he said, "And now, brethren, I come to my fourth and final point....". Dr. Matheson and my father were sitting just below the pulpit on the pulpit platform, and in a voice audible to those in the front but apparently not to the preacher, Dr. Matheson leant across to my father and wearily said, "Oh, Lang, that's another hour — at least!" And so it proved to be.

Dr. Matheson used to tease my father about his ecclesiastical parentage. One evening my father's sermon to a mainly working class congregation had tended to be far too academic and he had noted that his listeners had become restless. Afterwards in the vestry my father apologised to Dr. Matheson for attempting to be too scholarly. He was forgiven and the Doctor in his fine Scottish voice added, "You can't help it, Lang, it comes from your mother's milk and your father's ginger ale."

The four years my father had spent as assistant to Dr. Macleod and Dr. Matheson had taught him more about the ministry of the Church of Scotland and its purpose than he had learnt during all his years of university study. He was now ready to have a charge of his own and in 1895 he was elected to the parish of Old Meldrum in Aberdeenshire, neighbouring the parish of Fyvie in which his father and uncle (Gavin Lang) had been successively ministers.

Shortly after his induction he married, and my mother soon provided in the manse the happiest of homes where all their four children were born. Outside the rural town of Old Meldrum, the parish was scattered and mainly farming, and for a diligent minister like my father, it was difficult in those days to visit the furthest homes. At first he undertook his duties on foot, but when he found that his Free Church contemporary had acquired a modern bicycle which enabled him to make his visitations more frequently and more quickly, my father went one better and bought a motor bicycle, later adding to it a sidecar. While this method certainly increased the speed of his work, it correspondingly reduced the safety of himself and my mother. My father never had any notion how to handle matters mechanical. Later at Whittingehame when he got a car, even in those early days, one travelled with him in fear and trembling. He made his own rules of the road as he drove along, his basic rule being that on approaching a main road he would put his foot down hard on the accelerator and cross at speed because, as he said, "it stands to reason, the quicker you cross the road, the sooner you are out of danger". To offer to drive was almost more exasperating as he was the world's most critical back seat driver. To him every other driver was a danger on the road, and every pedestrian a fool. It was a great relief to the family that after his retirement the exigencies of the war deprived him of his car.

At Old Meldrum he was gaining the reputation of being a young minister of promise in the Church of Scotland. At a young age he had been invited to preach at some of the great city churches and he had had his invitation to appear before the King and Queen at Crathie. He certainly did not seek publicity as such invitations were often accepted reluctantly. In the pulpit or on the platform he would not show nervousness but to the end of his career he would face the big occasion with some trepidation. Marshall Lang was essentially a parish minister, well known and well beloved by all within its bounds, understanding the needs of his flock, both young and old. His lifelong interest in history and archaeology encouraged him to study the growth of each parish where he was minister. At Old Meldrum he wrote a short but comprehensive book about the life of the parish of Meldrum from the Reformation onwards, and at Whittingehame where he wrote "The Seven Ages of an East Lothian Parish" the book was recognised as a model for parish histories.

*   *   *

His next charge was St. John's (Cross) Parish Church, Dundee, where he went in 1909. There had been some misunderstanding about the church to which he was to go as there were two churches of the name of St.John's in Dundee, and a friend had said to him that he should not hesitate to accept the charge as the church of St. John's was one of the finest in the city. Going to Dundee to preach his trial sermon he was more than disappointed to find that the church, far from being handsome, was one of the barest barn-type buildings with an underground gas-smelling vestry. It transpired that his friend had confused this church with the United Free Church bearing the name of St. John (but without the "Cross"), a church quite entitled to the epithet he had given it. After the service he made it clear to the Kirk Session that a condition of his acceptance would be, in his own words, "This church goes, or I go within five years".

The appointment was made, the condition accepted and the response to build a new church was immediate. There were prolonged negotiations with the Town Council as Heritors, with the public bodies concerned in the removal of the church to a site in the west end of the city, and after strenuous fund raising efforts, the new Norman edifice was built at a cost of nearly £16,000 and was dedicated free of debt in September, 1914.

Meantime parish work continued while the church was being built and it seemed that the challenge of the great enterprise was a stimulus to congregational activity. A few months after the outbreak of the Great War in 1914 my father was called away to serve as chaplain to the forces, first in the Forth Coast Defence and latterly in the Aberdeen Coast Defence and this he continued to do until the end of the War. He tried to keep in touch with his congregation at St. John's (Cross) by visiting Dundee as often as he could but Sunday services had to be conducted by a succession of retired ministers. My mother and willing helpers in the congregation continued the parish work most of which was now directed towards the War effort.

At the end of the War my father was fifty, a critical age in the life of many ministers occupying city charges. Should he now continue at St. John's and perhaps end his ministry there or should he seek another appointment? He realised that as he grew older he would be less able to contribute to the work of a growing parish and also he would reduce his own chances of getting another and smaller charge. St. John's with its new church and young congregation, mainly from the expanding boundaries of Dundee, was, he felt, better suited to a younger man with his career ahead of him. The problem was settled for him when he was invited to apply for the vacant charge of Whittingehame Parish in East Lothian.

15. <u>M.B.L.</u> — Whittingehame and the Balfours

My father was inducted to the charge of Whittingehame in November 1918, where he continued as minister until his retirement in 1939. For him and my mother and their family it was an ideal rural parish, the largest in East Lothian, at the southern end reaching into the Lammermuir Hills and to the north covering rich arable and in parts finely wooded land with prosperous farms, and in the centre, the hub of parish activity, the house and grounds of Whittingehame, the home of the Balfours.[1] The scattered population of the parish when we arrived numbered around five hundred, the men and many of the women being mainly engaged in agriculture, and in those days of flourishing estate ownership a high proportion worked as gardeners (there were twelve at one time), foresters, game keepers and the domestic staff in the house.

As means of transport was limited, entertainment was mainly confined within the parish. The benevolent laird had provided a parish hall, frequently used for dances and concerts, and a bowling green brought success at county level to the bowlers of Whittingehame. To my father's gratification the church was always well attended.

The manse of Whittingehame, an elegant building of red sandstone, was ample in size for the requirements of our family and in it we spent a very happy, if somewhat austere, childhood. When first we went to Whittingehame there was no electricity, and in the winter my mother spent much of her time trimming the paraffin lamps and attending to the paraffin stoves. The nearest telephone was at Whittingehame House which we were welcome to use but did so reluctantly when Mr. Balfour was at home as we felt we might be interrupting more important calls from London when he was a cabinet minister. Our nearest shopping village and railway station were at East Linton, some three miles away, and at first our only means of transport was a pony trap. Looking back over the years, we may have overworked our two patient "all purpose" ponies, Molly and Jean. We certainly looked after them with great devotion,

---

1. Arthur James Balfour (1848-1930) was laird of Whittingehame for nearly half a century. A statesman and philosopher of great distinction, he held many of the highest offices of state during his lifetime and was Prime Minister from 1902 to 1905. He received the OM in 1916 and an earldom in 1922.

feeding and grooming them and cleaning out the stable, but in return we expected them to be on call to take my father at short notice to the furthest bounds of the parish or to gallop with us over an improvised race course round the glebe.

My father spent most of his time in the parish, always giving up his Saturdays to the preparation of his Sunday service and especially his sermon which was written but not closely read. He paid great attention to the content of his sermon, carefully collecting his material and presenting it clearly, logically and with a message that would leave his congregation in no doubt about the purpose of his discourse. He was not a fluent extempore preacher; he was never dramatic but some of the many hundreds of sermons he preached during his long ministry were of the highest standard. He did not reach the heights of oratory of his father or Archbishop brother, but he always took pride in what he had to say and would never allow his discourse to be unprepared or second rate. As a senior member of the Presbytery his contributions at their meetings were valued and when, often against his wishes, he was persuaded to take part in a church committee in Edinburgh, he was heard with the respect due to a man who had long experience in the Church. On two occasions he was commissioned to represent the Church of Scotland at commemorative celebrations in America and he greatly enjoyed his visits to New York and Pittsburgh and the opportunity to meet so many interesting people from all over the world. In 1930 he was granted the honorary degree of Doctor of Divinity by his own Alma Mater, Glasgow University, an honour which gave him great pleasure.

At Whittingehame there was time for him to pursue his lifelong interest in local history and archaeology, digging out material, both literally and metaphorically, which provided the contents for his book "The Seven Ages of an East Lothian Parish". The book was well received in historical circles as a model for parish histories. Acknowledging the book, Uncle Cosmo wrote from Lambeth on 18.12.29 "...it is really through these local histories that one is best able to get a conception of the whole history of the country; and I am very glad you have taken so large a share in this good work."

Lord Balfour wrote from London on 16.12.29.

"Dear Mr. Lang,
Many grateful thanks for the present of your book

containing the History of the Seven Ages of our Parish. It will perpetuate your memory as long as the Lowland Parishes continue to exist. May it be for all time!

All who are in any way connected with the history of the Scottish Lowlands will enjoy the fruits of your labours, and no one more sincerely than the present Laird of Whittingehame.

> With all good wishes for the New Year,
> Believe me,
> Yours very truly,
>
> Balfour."

*   *   *

But the absorbing interest to him and to us all at Whittingehame was the Balfour family. The Balfours came to Whittingehame early in the nineteenth century and were the descendants of the Balfours of Balbirnie, Fife. It was probably not known to them that my father, the minister of Whittingehame, was also a descendant, through his grandmother, of a Balfour of Balbirnie, as he was the great ($\times$ 4) grandson of the Miss Balfour of Balbirnie who had eloped with the village shoemaker, Adam Stobie, in the seventeenth century.

Arthur James Balfour, afterwards Lord Balfour, was the laird of Whittingehame and when he was in residence he was supreme in more ways than one. When absent in London, Miss Alice Balfour, his sister, was the kindly and prevailing spirit of the parish. They took an interest in the minister and his family and Miss Balfour would frequently visit the manse, Mr. Balfour only occasionally. Their kindness and consideration to us were unbounded, giving us the use of one of their tennis courts, annually inviting us to Christmas parties and delivering to the manse baskets laden with fruit and vegetables from the spacious gardens. We were allowed a free run of the beautiful grounds of Whittingehame House and if we were fortunate enough to meet Mr. Balfour at any time he would always stop and talk to us. Although he had the reputation of having his head in the clouds, in his conversation with us he would quickly return to earth and would never talk down to us. One of the highlights of my youth, at the age of sixteen, was an introduction by a local Member of Parliament to the gallery of the House of Commons where I listened to a debate on India. Sometime later I met Mr. Balfour walking in the grounds and I told him how I had listened to a debate in the House of Commons. He seemed interested and when I said I had heard Mr. Amery, at that time the Colonial and Dominion Secretary of State, he raised his hands and explained, "What a pity! Poor Amery, such a dull speaker but usually very sound. What impression did you get?" I have no recollection now of my mumbled reply but I have certainly not forgotten the day when a former Prime Minister asked my opinion about the performance of one of his Cabinet colleagues!

When the Balfours were in residence, they regularly attended the Sunday morning service. It was not only the presence of Mr. Balfour that made the service an ordeal for my father, it was also the galaxy of kindly critical talent that filled the Balfour pew that added to his anxiety. At times there were as many as twenty Balfour visitors at church including Gerald, Arthur's brother, a Fellow of Trinity College, Cambridge and a lesser philosopher and statesman; his sister, Mrs. Sidgwick, Principal of Newnham College, Cambridge; another sister, Lady Rayleigh, the wife of a Nobel Prize Winner; his niece, Mrs. Dugdale, Balfour's official biographer; and not least, his sister-in-law, Lady Frances Balfour, a daughter of the Duke of Argyll, often a stormy petrel, a suffragist, and a most staunch Presbyterian. It was she who would conclude her letters to my father with the words, "Please give my best wishes to your family — provided they are Presbyterian" — no doubt a dig at my father's archiepiscopal brother. It was known to us in the manse that my father's sermon often became the topic of conversation at Sunday lunch at Whittingehame House and it would be difficult to find a family who could equal the Balfours in erudite discussion. The Balfours were kindly and said little but praise; Lady Frances was more openly critical. It was not unusual for a footman to arrive at the manse late on a Sunday afternoon with a letter from Lady Frances questioning some point in my father's sermon or criticising an item on the praise list as being inappropriate for the subject of his address. Their presence in the pew would last for six or eight Sundays in the year and when it was known that the house party had returned to London, the news was greeted with a sigh of relief.

One outstanding event during my father's ministry at Whittingehame happened in the summer of 1922 when Mr. Balfour, at the close of the Coalition Government, had as his guests Lord Birkenhead, Mr. Lloyd George, Sir Robert Horne, then Chancellor of the Exchequer, and other less notable persons. To the parish church they were led by Mr. Balfour on the Sunday morning, naturally creating a stir among the local folk. Lord Birkenhead had walked to the entrance gate of the churchyard but had gone no further, apologising to my father afterwards that regretfully he had started from the house without his proper Sunday clothes and had thought it disrespectful to attend the service. My father had preached a non-committal sermon usual at a time of political perplexity which had pleased Mr. Lloyd George, the leader of the Coalition. "I think he's one of us," he whispered to Miss Balfour at the conclusion of the sermon. I remember to this day the praise being led by the little Welshman in a loud and high pitched tenor which reached above the voices of the congregation.

That afternoon my parents were invited to tea at Whittingehame House to meet the distinguished guests, and my father, in a note recording the occasion, tells how the conversation at tea had turned on the behaviour of Mary, Queen of Scots. Not surprising in such company there was plenty of discussion and differences of opinion were expressed. Miss Balfour, a lady of strict propriety, supported by Mr. Lloyd George, so strongly defended the actions of the Queen that Lord Birkenhead was prompted to remark, "It seems, Miss Balfour, that you and Mr. Lloyd George encourage the same standards of morality."

Lord Balfour died in 1930 and his sister a few years later and with their passing the glory of these days largely departed. Whittingehame House was sold and since then has changed hands several times. The beautiful gardens, now so neglected, are almost unrecognisable, only the magnificant trees remaining as a memorial to happier days. Lord Balfour and his sister were buried in the ancient, now private, burial ground near the old castle of Whittingehame. Lord Balfour's funeral service was conducted by my father and was for him a memorable occasion, not just because the little church was crowded with some of the most distinguished of the land but more so because my father was glad of the opportunity to remember Lord Balfour for his kindness and his inspiration to him and his parish and for their close friendship. At the conclusion, he offered a prayer of thanks expressing the feelings of his own people at Whittingehame and of the whole nation:

"for those gifts of heart and mind by which Lord

Balfour had enriched the world, hindered the forces of evil, advanced the kingdom of truth, righteousness, goodwill and peace in the world by his service to our Country and Empire and to the peoples and nations beyond our shores."

A. J. Balfour with Lloyd George at Whittingehame Church.

16. M.B.L. — The Moderator and Retirement

In 1935 a newspaper headline read "Country Minister becomes Moderator". Thus the Church of Scotland recognised the work of my father, granting him its highest honour, the Moderator of its General Assembly. In true Presbyterian manner the General Assembly of the Church of Scotland elects its own Moderator on the nomination of an influential committee of senior ministers. Sometimes the choice is a minister of renowned scholarship, more often a leader in the corridors of power of church government, and very occasionally a minister with distinguished overseas service is honoured. My father was none of these. He was essentially a good parish minister. Supporting his election, Dr. Norman Maclean, at one time one of Scotland's leading churchmen, wrote:

> "The great work of the Church of Scotland is not done in the Committee Rooms of 121 George Street or in the General Assembly. It is done in quiet country parishes by ministers who serve and look for no earthly reward. The inspiration of a crowd, the applause of the multitude, come not their way. They are content to serve anonymously. They minister to the primary workers who carry the cities on their backs. Without the fresh young life coming into the cities from the country parishes, the cities would soon atrophy. In the past the Church of Scotland was careful to honour the country ministers by raising some of them to the Moderator's chair of the Assembly . . . It is now well nigh a quarter of a century since the last country minister was called to the chair in the Church of Scotland Assembly. If that good rule was not to be forgotten, the time had come for the Church to select a Moderator from the country once more. And no happier choice could be made than that of the Minister of the largest parish in East Lothian, the classic parish of Whittingehame.[1]"

It would certainly not have escaped the notice of the nomination committee that my father came from a family with a long and proud

---

1. In this century there have been three Moderators from serving ministers of Whittingehame, Dr. James Robertson in 1909, Dr. Marshall Lang in 1935 and Dr. Roy Sanderson in 1967.

record in the Church of Scotland. His father had been Moderator, likewise two of his uncles by marriage; his wife's grandfather had been a Moderator and many other relatives had served the Church faithfully and with merit. And perhaps the committee were also not unmindful of the fact that an elder brother was occupying the Chair of Saint Augustine of Canterbury and a younger brother was the Assistant Bishop of Peterborough.

*   *   *

So when my father became Moderator on 21st May 1935, he knew very well what was expected of him and he performed his duties with eminence and dignity. He was 67 when he had allowed his name to go forward to the Nomination Committee, not without some hesitation as he felt that the intensive strain of a Moderator's year might be too much for him. But he and my mother stood up to the strain remarkably well, fulfilling the great variety of their duties to the satisfaction and pleasure of the many they met. My father was glad when the Assembly was over. To perform the courtesies of the Assembly was no problem to him but he was certainly not the first Moderator to be baffled at times by the complexities of procedure and debate. There was one day he enjoyed especially which was unique in the annals of the Church when my father, the Moderator, invited his brother, the Archbishop, to address the Assembly. Receiving him officially from the chair, my father clasped his brother's hand and with a broad smile and just the suspicion of a wink addressed him in the proper manner as "Your Grace". There was a burst of laughter from the Assembly followed by prolonged cheers in recognition of this memorable occasion.

As Moderator he had to fulfill an endless programme of duties, presbyteries to be visited, sermons and addresses to be delivered on great occasions including one from the pulpit of Westminster Abbey which he claimed was the first time it had been occupied by a presbyterian minister, many impromptu talks at all sorts of times and in all sorts of places, a few words to miners down a coal mine and to the players after a Scottish League football match. His foreign tour took him to Egypt and the Sudan where he was warmly received not only by the Scots abroad but also by people of other nationalities and other faiths.

*   *   *

My father and mother.

At the age of 71 when my father retired from the parish of Whittingehame, my parents bought a small house in its own grounds in Gifford, East Lothian, a picturesque village a few miles from Edinburgh, where they lived happily and in good health for fourteen years. They delighted in the company of their many friends and were always to pleased to welcome to their home their children and an increasing number of grandchildren. For my father, retirement meant the enjoyment of as many years of leisure as his span of life would allow. He read a lot, he began writing his reminiscences which sadly were never completed as he found concentration more difficult as he grew older; he did light work in the garden, and regularly exercised their old English sheep dog, Tweed. For my mother, there was always work to be done in the house, probably at times too much for her age as one domestic problem seemed to follow another. She often seemed tired, but she never complained of ill health. One afternoon in the early summer of 1954 when my father came from the garden carrying a bunch of the first roses, he found my mother dead in her

chair, a terrible shock from which he never recovered. It was not
until after her death that he fully realised how much he had
depended upon her during the fifty-seven years of their married life.

While my father inherited the characteristics of the Langs, my
mother had the good down-to-earth qualities of the Farquharsons, of
practicality and sound common sense. Like her brother and sisters
she could at times appear abrupt and anything fanciful would be
dismissed as nonsense. She was always capable of a deep affection for
her family although she would resist any demonstration of such
feelings. She had certainly greater patience and often more
understanding than my father, so much so that my sisters and I soon
learnt that the best approach to my father in order to solve amicably
a family problem was first of all to explain the position to her.

My father died four months after my mother and was buried
beside her in the churchyard of Whittingehame.

*   *   *

Like his father before him, my father regarded himself first and
foremost as a parish minister of the Church of Scotland, believing
that the parish was the unit of his mission. Although there were times
in his long ministry when greatness was thrust upon him, he did not
seek the highlights of his calling, but when they came to him he was
always glad to return afterwards to the parochial scene.

Towards the end of his life he began to witness changes in the
Church of Scotland, the closure of churches, the amalgamation of
parishes and, what hurt him most of all, a fall in membership and in
the number of ministers, and he was reluctant to accept what was
inevitable. He was essentially a man of his generation and found it
difficult to adjust himself to the modern scene.

In the family circle he was held in highest regard, at times almost
with some awe. By nature somewhat reserved and seldom completely
relaxed, it was not until his family grew older that they fully
understood his true merits and were able to talk freely to him and
share his companionship. He had an endless store of tales, usually
based on his own experiences, which were told to visitors to the
manse, becoming more exaggerated as the years passed and often
corrected by my mother with her love of accuracy and somewhat to
the annoyance of my father. But differences of opinion in the family
and between my father and mother were superficial, and for more

than half a century they lived a very happy life together which they shared with their children.

There were four in the family, Hannah Hamilton Marshall (1897-1976) who married William Smith Ramsay Henderson, at first an officer in the Indian Army and later a farmer and hotel proprietor; Annie Laurina (1901-1982) who married Harry Alexander Macdonald, latterly a colonel in the Royal Engineers; Margaret Eleanor Farquharson (1905-1967) who married Robert Holms-Kerr Hope, an East Lothian farmer; and William Farquharson Marshall (1908-), a Sudan civil servant, who married Sheila Clive Parker.

17. <u>Hannah Buchanan Lang</u>

<u>Hannah Buchanan Lang</u> (<u>1872-1952</u>) — Aunt Hannah — the sixth of the family and the only daughter of John Marshall and Hannah Lang, spent the early years of her life in Glasgow helping her mother in the many activities associated with the busy parish of the Barony. She had been christened Hannah after her mother and grandmother Keith and Buchanan after her maternal grandfather, Archibald Buchanan. By the naming of their children, my grandparents had ensured that the family names of Marshall and Keith, Hamilton and Buchanan would at least be perpetuated in their generation; the only two who could not claim family connections in their names were Cosmo Gordon and Norman Macleod, the former called after the Laird of Fyvie and the latter after my grandfather's immediate predecessor in the Barony, one of a long line of famous Church of Scotland ministers. It may be of some interest to Sassenachs to note that the two who rose to high office in the Church of England bore distinctive names of Scottish origin. There seems to be no obvious reason, other than family connection, why my father and his elder sister should successively have borne the name Buchanan unless it was to underline the fact that the Langs could claim a clan connection. Archibald Buchanan, my great-grandfather, and his nephew, James, were prominent members of the Buchanan Society, one of them becoming its President. My father claimed that he was one of the Clan Buchanan and that I was entitled to wear the Buchanan tartan, but when I reached an age to wear the kilt, I am glad that my mother's wishes prevailed and that I was able to wear the less flamboyant tartan of the Farquharson clan.

In the summer of 1891 a young minister of great promise arrived in Glasgow to assist my grandfather at the Barony. He came from St. Andrews and his name was Robert Barclay (1869-1904) — Uncle Bertie. He had been at the university for seven years in order to become a Master of Arts and a Bachelor of Divinity and during that time was the life and soul of student activity, a man of robust health and highest spirits. Andrew Lang (no relation) wrote of him, "He was happy as a matter of principle, no less than as a result of temperament, and was the cause of happiness in others." His talents took him in many directions; he was an able, but not outstanding, scholar, he was a raconteur par excellence, a generous host and a good companion, a fine sportsman and a particularly good golfer, added to which he had the promise of becoming an eloquent preacher. At golf his long game was straight and accurate but the weakness of his game was his inability to sink short putts. Preaching in St. Andrews one Sunday he caught the eye of Tom Morris in the congregation. "Man, ye missed nae short putts to-day," was Morris' comment after the service.

After graduation he acted as assistant at the Parish Church of St. Andrews and would happily have stayed there in the comparative leisure of the parish enjoying the company of so many of his friends and living within a short approach of the Old Course of St. Andrews had it had not been that Dr. Boyd, the minister of St. Andrews, advised him otherwise. "Fondness of St. Andrews is one thing," he said, "but this is a working world."

And by going to the Barony, he was thrown into the deep end of the working world. He found exhausting parish work visiting the congregation in the tenements of Glasgow. He took his share in the services and preaching, but, as he said, he valued "more than words could express, the training and the inspiration of loving counsel and guidance" he had received from my grandfather.

*　　　*　　　*

It was a true romance, but not original, that caused the lively young assistant to fall in love with the minister's beautiful daughter. This is just what happened. Robert Barclay was 24 and Hannah Lang only 21, but they were in no position to marry immediately as the stipend of an assistant minister was less than meagre. In a sense fortune favoured their romance. Robert's father, the minister of the West Kirk and Parish of Greenock, died suddenly in 1893 and the patrons and kirk session of Greenock decided that they could do no better than invite to the charge the son of the minister who had served them so faithfully for many years. So Robert was duly inducted as the minister of the senior church of the growing city of Greenock and two years later he married Hannah Lang.

The nine years of his ministry at Greenock were devoted to tireless work in the parish. Although she was always somewhat delicate, Aunt Hannah played her part in the parish, but she rightly felt that her first duty was to provide a quiet resting place for her ever active husband. Their only child, Dorothy, was born in 1898, but the joy of her birth was shadowed by sickness in the family. The final tragedy of Uncle Bertie's sudden and premature death in a dentist's chair on January 30th, 1904, three days after his thirty-fifth birthday, broke Aunt Hannah's life.

Although she outlived her husband by nearly half a century, she never really recovered from the shock of his untimely death. She always carried a well worn photograph of him in her handbag and was irritated when a photographer declined to alter his Victorian posture and features to bring the picture up to date. After his death she lived for a short time in Aberdeen with her parents and then bought a small house in Ann Street, Edinburgh, where she and Dorothy lived for some years, later moving south to London when Dorothy went "on the stage". Dorothy had many of the qualities of her father; she was lively, vivacious, theatrical, a wonderful story-teller and a great mimic, and on the stage she played some minor parts in London theatres until she married Neville Harvey, a naval officer, in 1925.

During the war, Aunt Hannah left London and joined Dorothy and her family in Bath, but the stresses and anxieties of the war strained family relationships to the limit so that as soon as she could she returned to a private hotel in South Kensington, joining the other widows and elderly spinsters who seem to support these establishments. Another great sadness in the life of Aunt Hannah was the death of Dorothy in 1944 at the age of 46. She was not only her one devoted child but after Bertie's death she saw so much in her character to remind her of her beloved husband. So far as she was able she enjoyed living in London, being visited frequently by her brothers and their families but she was always faced with the anxiety of trying to live within a small income at a time of rising costs. When she was no longer able to look after herself, she moved to a nursing home in Wimbledon where she died in 1952 in her eightieth year.

*   *   *

To those of us who knew her in her old age, Aunt Hannah was a dear, gentle lady who had suffered much sadness in her life and bravely bore her sorrows. She did not appear to be a very forceful character and was probably dominated by her husband during the nine years of their marriage but like her brothers she held firmly to her convictions, sometimes to a degree of obstinacy. The passionate admiration which she had for Bertie continued throughout her life and "Memories" of him which she recalled so affectionately in her book of that title was circulated privately to her family and friends. It would be difficult to find someone who had a more Presbyterian background than Aunt Hannah; her father and both her grandfathers, her husband and her father-in-law were all ministers of the Church of Scotland; but nevertheless after Bertie's death she found comfort and consolation in the doctrines of Anglo-Catholicism. It was certainly her faith and her devotion for her family that kept her going without complaint and often with good humour to the end of her days.

18. Norman Macleod Lang, DD

<u>Norman Macleod</u> (<u>1875-1956</u>) — Uncle Norman — followed in the footsteps of his elder brother, Cosmo, into the priesthood of the Church of England. Although professionally and intellectually there were similarities between the two brothers and they had a closer bond of friendship with one another than with any of their other brothers, there was a distinct difference in much of their character. Like Cosmo, Norman proceeded to Oxford after a few years at Glasgow University. A friend who remembered him at Oxford wrote about him after his death. As an undergraduate at Christ Church College in 1896, he recalls how a contemporary don once said, "How well I remember Norman coming to the House; handsome, popular,

Norman Macleod Lang, the Bishop.

vivacious, clever, possessed of a lovely speaking and singing voice, but not industrious — had he been he might well have matched his illustrious elder brother Cosmo." Norman had no ambition to hold office in the politics of university life, nor was he an athlete of any merit, he was "just a bit of a lad at Oxford" as he described himself in his undergraduate days. But if he never allowed himself to over-work, he left Oxford with a good degree and went on to Cuddeston to train for the priesthood.

After ordination at the age of twenty-five, Norman joined Cosmo at Portsea as one of the vicar's team of young progressive curates and was subjected to the frugality and discipline of the vicarage with no preferential treatment being given to a younger brother. He worked at Portsea for nearly four years and then went to South Africa, first to become a curate of Blomfontein Cathedral and later the vicar of Kronstandt. What attracted him to South Africa is not known. Douglas his elder brother, by this time married and well established in the country, may have persuaded him to come out to South Africa to help in the development of the colonial diocese of the episcopal church after the South African War. But his stay there was short-lived as he returned to England in 1906 to marry Monica Crossfield, the daughter of a wealthy Liverpool industrialist with property in Hampshire, and to take his bride to London where he was inducted as the curate of Christ Church, Lancaster Gate. Three years later his next move was to Leicester to become the vicar of the Cathedral Church of St. Martin's and in 1913 he was appointed Bishop Suffragan of Leicester, a position which he held for fourteen years. With the division of the diocese of Peterborough in 1927, Uncle Norman was deprived of the suffraganship of Leicester and was appointed Assistant Bishop of Peterborough and Archdeacon of Northampton. The loss of his style and title of Bishop of Leicester hurt him deeply.

Some years earlier in 1918 he had suffered a very grievous personal loss when his wife died. She had been an invalid for some years and finally became the victim of the influenza epidemic of that year. Their brief marriage of nine years had been blissfully happy. Monica will be remembered as a very charming lady and although latterly handicapped by ill health she was a wonderful hostess for her husband. A light went out in Norman's life when Monica died and he became — in appearance but not in vigour or grip — prematurely old.

He retired in 1947 after giving his life for nearly half a century to the ministry of the Church of England. Those who knew him during these years remember him as an administrator of considerable ability, concerning himself especially with the maintenance of the many ancient and historic churches in the diocese; as a preacher, one of his contemporaries wrote, "he was in his day unsurpassed — forceful, fiery, prophetic; and who will ever forget his reading of the daily lessons in the Cathedral".

*   *   *

After his retirement, Uncle Norman lived for nearly ten years in the Rectory of Wappenham, near Towcester, a substantial house with a large garden. He never complained of being lonely although many thought that he was; he interested himself in village life and delighted in entertaining old friends, regaling them with his humour and his stories of earlier years. He enjoyed reading, and working hard in his garden and was always willing to offer his services voluntarily to help out in neighbouring parishes. "We are still without a rector," he once wrote when he was assisting during a local vacancy, "and I am still guinea-pigging, the pig without the guineas!" There had been a long and close friendship between himself and his housekeeper, Edith, who had been with him for over thirty years, looking after him with wonderful care and devotion. When her eyesight began to fail and she became increasingly arthritic, he did what he could to share with her the domestic work of the house.

More than anyone else Norman understood his distinguished brother, Cosmo. He admired Cosmo's ability and success, but was the first to recognise his more exasperating ways; Cosmo admired Norman's brain and would frequently turn to him for his views on the progress and problems which he faced in his high office. When he visited London, Norman stayed at Lambeth and the two brothers would welcome a tête-à-tête, discussing at length and late into the night the affairs of church and state. How far they reached agreement is speculative or how far advice was accepted is doubtful, as Norman would never disclose the opinion of his enigmatic brother. But there is no doubt they loved one another's company. Norman usually spent Christmas at Bishopthorpe or Lambeth and he looked forward to his annual visit to Ballure where they would so happily tramp the hills together.

*   *   *

During his years at Wappenham, Uncle Norman enjoyed a close friendship with his niece, my sister Laurina, and her family. Harry Macdonald, her Royal Engineer husband, had been posted near Wappenham after the war and almost by chance the Macdonald family met Uncle Norman and formed a friendship which was to continue to the end of his days. Uncle Norman was a regular and entertaining letter-writer. A selection of extracts from his letters to my sister after the Macdonald family had returned to Scotland reveal his sensitive nature, his humour and his great humanity.

He had been a lover of the Scottish Highlands since his youth when the family left the grime of Glasgow to spend their annual holiday on the West Coast of Scotland. In his letters he wrote rapturously about the beauties of the scenery, often illustrating his descriptions with delightful pen sketches of the mountains and the lochs he had loved so well, showing an artistic talent which he shared with his brothers and sometimes excelled.

"Yes, I know the dear little pub at Brig of Orchy", he wrote, "The last time I was there was for breakfast: in solitary majesty before anyone was down. An early start from Crianlarich, then my HQ and a kind colonel man gave me a lift by car as I wanted to explore the Black Mount, a bit from Inveroran. From there, too, starts the old Drovers' Road through Glencoe, which is fun. I'm told they have cut an awful lot of timber round Loch Tulla. There are some fine trees left of the primeval forest. The worst of the Black Mount from this end is that you have to tramp such miles of rough moor before getting to your climb, and start half exhausted. Loch Baa and Rannoch Moor always fascinate me — so primitive, yet friendly, non-human without being in-human (as some of Glencoe is)."

And he recalls in another letter a near-fatality of his youth:

"Your wee holiday makes my mouth water. All the dear old places, familiar in boyhood. Crainlarich, Loch Fyne, Loch Awe. It was Loch Fyne that nearly cut short my humble career. We had a house one summer at

Strachur, your dad a student at Glasgow, Cosmo at
Balliol, me a kid of 10 or 12. These two bathed from a
boat and when drying lurched the boat, and in I went.
Sank to the bottom — not missed! came up, sank again!
Then Cosmo managed to grab me by the hair, and pulled
me in. He often used to say afterwards that your dad's
contribution to my rescue was to sit in the bow of the boat
and pray!"

Transport was always a problem for Uncle Norman. Like his
brothers he had no knowledge, nor did he wish to acquire it, of the
workings of a machine and his total disregard for the hazards of the
road was the subject of innumerable stories. His impetuosity on a
motor cycle and later on as the driver of a car was proverbial. When
he retired and his range of interests became more local, he returned
to the ordinary bicycle to which later he had an engine fitted, but
that was not to last long. At the age of seventy-five he wrote,

> "In my senility, I thought it would be a thing to have
> a motor engine on my push-bike and save leg work. I got
> fed up with the beastly thing: it upset the balance of my
> bike and every time I got on, I fell off the other side, and
> every time I got off, I fell off on that side: then a plug that
> was always dirty, and petrol and oil to be mixed in the
> tank, a messy business. So it has come off again, and once
> again I have restored to me a perfectly good bike instead
> of an unreliable snort."

In most of his letters, he wrote of familiar things, about his life
in the village, his friends, his anxiety about Edith, kind enquiries
about Laurina and her family and about his brothers and sister and
their families; only very occasionally did he allow himself to express
deeper thoughts, as he did once when he wrote after Easter in 1950.

> "Easter is over: at least the mere observance — itself
> is never over. I suppose that even in your schismatic
> country there is some small notice of it beyond the
> holiday! Our church is lovely with daffodils and forsythia
> and cyclamens and many beautiful things — to tell us that
> He who "came down from Heaven and was Incarnate and
> Crucified and Risen" was the Lord of all Nature, too, like
> us, will be redeemed, remade, cured of blemishes, no

more "red in tooth and claw" — the New Heavens and the New Earth, but remade out of the old, for eternal loveliness. Isn't that more true than the dreary things some tell us, that the Earth will be frozen into sterility or burned up to ashes? and with it is a lovely thought when you smile at the little things perking up in your garden or watch the first exquisite green on trees and shrubs and hedgerows."

Uncle Norman died at Wappenham on May 5th 1956, at the age of eighty, a kind and friendly man with great good humour and abundant humanity.

19. David Marshall Lang

David Marshall (1876-1925) — Uncle David — the eighth and youngest child of the family of John Marshall and Hannah Lang, was born and brought up in Glasgow. Although physically he was fairly robust, he had no inclination towards intellectual pursuits and lacked the ability to continue his education beyond basic standards. When he grew older he found employment from time to time, but there was little continuity in any of his work. During the first World War he was passed fit for service and was drafted into the Pioneer Corps for a short period, proudly wearing the uniform of His Majesty's Forces. Sometime after the war he lived in Moffat, Dumfriesshire, with a Mr. and Mrs. Johnston, a kindly couple, who gave him a very comfortable home and introduced him to the life of the village where he played bowls for a local team and regularly attended the local church. He spent his holidays with my parents at Whittingehame and it was during one of these summers that he fell ill and died suddenly

A sister and four brothers: Hannah, Patrick, Cosmo, Douglas and Marshall.

in an Edinburgh nursing home at the age of forty-nine. He was buried in Warriston Cemetery, Edinburgh, beside many of my mother's Farquharson relatives.

As a schoolboy I remember Uncle David's visits to Whittingehame, going long and rather silent walks together and pitching and putting at golf for hours on the lawns of the manse. He was shy and unassuming, ill at ease in the company of strangers, but with those he knew well, he enjoyed the simple life which he understood.

*   *   *

At a family wedding in 1937 there was a brief reunion of five of the six surviving members of my grandparents' family, Patrick, Cosmo and Douglas now in their seventies and Marshall and Hannah in their late sixties. Norman, the youngest, was unfortunately the only absentee. The passing of the years had been kind to them; in

Marshall, Patrick and Douglas.

appearance they had inherited the distinction of their father and in character the wit and humour of their mother, and these qualities they had retained into old age. It was nearly half a century since they had lived together in 5 Woodlands Terrace, Glasgow, before they went their several ways and their paths had only infrequently crossed during that time. But on that summer afternoon they seemed to relive some of the close companionship of their earlier years. Patrick, now very much the doyen of the family, lightheartedly sought to assert the influence of his position as the head of the family; Cosmo, on this occasion relaxing just a little from the dignity of his office, challenged as he had done in his youth any authority from his elder brother; Douglas, with that mischievous look in his eye, was prepared to remove any of his brothers from their pedestals; Marshall, perhaps the most orthodox of the family, retained a distinct presbyterian presence and Hannah, allowing herself just a little self-pity, enjoyed to the full the affectionate care and attention of her brothers. Over the years they had always been a very humane and remarkable family and continued to be so to the end of their days.

THE FARQUHARSONS OF FINZEAN
1. Donald Farquharson of Tillygarmond

Donald Farquharson of Castleton, Braemar, acquired the lands of Tillygarmond in the parish of Birse in 1579 and was the first Farquharson to establish a foothold in this region of Aberdeenshire. Donald was the eldest son of Finla Mor, the Scottish standard bearer who was killed at the battle of Pinkie in 1547. Donald's mother, Beatrice Garden of Banchory-Devenick and Finla Mor's second wife, had an exceptionally fine voice and often entertained Mary Queen of Scots. To express her delight the queen presented Beatrice with a harp, said to have belonged to the queen's mother, Mary of Lorraine. The harp is still to be seen in the National Museum of Antiquities in Edinburgh.

Tillygarmond had previously been occupied for two years by Robert Hog, a burgess of Aberdeen. Some records maintain he was so heavily indebted to the Farquharsons that in repayment of his debt he gave them the lands of Tillygarmond. A charter entitling Donald Farquharson to Tillygarmond was granted by the Bishop of Aberdeen on 4th February 1580, the charter threatening severe fines by the superior, the Bishop, if adequate steps were not taken to preserve game on the land.

The first Donald was succeeded by his son, also Donald, younger of Tillygarmond, in 1603. The young Donald had married in 1599 and had five sons and five daughters. The two elder sons, Donald and Robert, acquired respectively the lands of Monaltrie and Whitehouse and became the progenitors of those branches of the Farquharson clan.

The younger Donald continued to be the laird of Tillygarmond until 1628. Meantime his eldest son, Robert, had acquired by charter in the year 1609, the property of Finzean, at that time the area around the site of the present Finzean House and the neighbouring farms and woodlands. Thus for a short period two Farquharsons were lairds of adjacent properties, Donald of Tillygarmond and Robert his son, of Finzean.

The younger Donald could hardly have found sufficient interests to occupy his time at Tillygarmond. At the invitation of the Earl of Huntly he was appointed the Earl's bailie for Strathdee and Strathaven. Donald seemed to have had a restless nature, his energies often being directed towards the irregular warlike pursuits of his time. During the civil war, Donald supported the cause of King

Charles against Cromwell and took a prominent part in local feuds and plundering expeditions. It was shortly after raiding the lands of Alexander Strachan of Glenkindie that Donald eventually met his end. Strachan was a prominent Covenanter and combining courage and cunning he carried off a great quality of muskets, pikes and other armour from the servants of Donald Farquharson as they were being brought from Aberdeen to Donald's home. Donald retaliated by raiding and laying waste the lands and property of Alexander Strachan at Glenkindie, an act for which Strachan sought revenge. Some time later Donald Farquharson joined the army of the Earl of Montrose to fight for the Royalist causes and it was while Montrose and his troops were in Aberdeen that Donald met his fate. One night, accompanied by a party of young Royalist revellers, Donald and his friends broke camp and "fearless and careless of the enemy" set out to enjoy themselves in Aberdeen. On the 15th March 1645, late in the evening they were set upon and outnumbered by a band of Convenanters among whom was said to be Strachan, and Donald was killed in the fray. Donald's death was a irreparable loss as he was one of the best of Montrose's lieutenants. "One of the noblest captains among all the Highland men of Scotland", wrote Spalding. He is buried in the Laird of Drum's aisle in St. Nicholas Church, Aberdeen.

2. The Early Lairds of Finzean — 1609-1786

Years of Expansion

Robert Farquharson, the eldest of the six sons of Donald
Farquharson of Tilliegarmond, became the first laird of Finzean
(1609-1632) on 11th May 1609, when the lands of Finzean were
granted to him by charter by the Bishop of Aberdeen. Previously, but
for only three years, Finzean had been the property of Sir Alexander
Gordon of Cluny. Before that Sir Robert Carnegie had been the
owner for about fifty years.

A year before he became laird, Robert had married Margaret
McIntosh, an interesting link with an earlier generation as Robert's
grandfather was known as Donald Farquharson alias McIntosh of
Castleton of Braemar, a descendant of the Shaw branch of the
McIntoshes who came over from Rothiemurchus and settled in
Braemar. Robert and Margaret had four sons, Alexander, Robert,
William and Donald and so far as is known only one daughter,
Isabella.

In their marriages the wives of the first three Farquharson lairds
produced fifteen sons and in every generation there was a repetition
of names, making the task of the genealogist all the more difficult.
The names of Donald, Robert and William seem to have been the
choice of every Farquharson family at that time. There were
daughters too but shamefully in this respect the records are
incomplete unless the daughter happened to marry a man of
property. But it was more than just virility that caused the almost
perpetual pregnancy of their wives; their husbands also had in mind
succession and the acquisition of more and more land. Six of the
seven lairds of Finzean between the years of 1609 and 1793 added
territory to the estate; the seventh, poor Francis, had little
opportunity as he was laird for less than a year (1786). Not only did
the lairds purchase land, some of them also gained property through
marriage. Migvie in Cromar, a large property owned by the Finzean
Farquharsons for some three hundred years, came into their
possession through the marriage of Alexander, the second laird, with
the family of Keith.

The map of West Aberdeenshire in the seventeenth and
eighteenth centuries became like a jigsaw puzzle, each piece adding
yet another property to some branch of the Farquharson clan, until

about 1850 when the picture was complete and the whole area was virtually Farquharson territory. But the situation was not to last for long. During the latter half of the nineteenth century wealth created in the Industrial Revolution spread north, and highland estates were purchased by commercial magnates from the south. They built large mansions in the Scottish baronial style although they could make no claim to a Scottish barony. They assumed the title of laird although this was often reluctantly accepted by their tenants and estate workers, and they wore a kilt with a tartan of their own design. But times were changing, as indeed they keep on changing, and most of the new proprietors brought much-needed wealth to Aberdeenshire. They improved the buildings, the farm land and the woodlands of their properties and they attracted to Deeside many people from the south who enjoyed the scenery and the sport, and were prepared to pay for their pleasure.

The Farquharsons of Finzean had little or no industrial connection; they were professional, landowning people and did not have the means to spread themselves like many of their new-found neighbours. They disposed of some of their property about the middle of the nineteenth century and thereafter tended to concentrate their interests in Finzean although Migvie and Lumphanan continued to be part of the estate until 1936. Only a few Deeside lairds can claim such direct Scottish inheritance as the Farquharsons of Finzean and they have retained their "Scottishness" by the education of their children in Scottish schools, by residing on the estate and by taking an active and interested part in local affairs.

*   *   *

Robert Farquharson and his son, <u>Alexander the second laird</u> (<u>1632-1666</u>) added the farms of Percie, Balnaboth and Balnahard to the estate and later Alexander acquired the Mill of Clinter and Dalsack.

*   *   *

Francis succeeded Alexander, his father, as <u>third laird of Finzean</u> (<u>1666-1707</u>) and was laird for forty-one years. He married Margaret Arbuthnot, a daughter of the laird of Findowrie, Angus, a happy departure from precedent as the Farquharsons had previously taken their brides from neighbouring estates in Aberdeenshire. During this long period as laird, Francis made a very considerable contribution to the development of the estate. Like his father and grandfather before him he extended the lands of Finzean by adding the farm of Whitestone to the estate in 1681. On 16th April in the same year, he acquired by charter about a mile and a half of salmon fishing on the south bank of the River Dee below the Forest of Lendrum, a stretch of river called the Commonty Water that has provided excellent sport for the lairds of Finzean and their guests for the last three hundred years. Apart from one Finzean pool at the top end of the stretch, the river has been shared between Finzean and the neighbouring estate of Ballogie, a joint ownership enjoyed by the estates for very many years. The ownership of the Commonty was challenged by the Crown in 1932 and was the subject of a prolonged and celebrated law suit which fortunately for the two estates was decided in their favour.

When the Farquharsons went to Finzean in the early years of the seventeenth century there must have been a house for them to occupy but there seems to be no trace of this early dwelling. Francis built a new house, in no sense a pretentious mansion but a type of "Ha' Hoose", typical of the period, facing east and west with substantial stone walls to keep out the wind and possible invaders from the Forest of Birse, a house very much in keeping with the size of property that the Farquharsons of Finzean then owned. Finzean House has undergone many changes since then but a wall of the house that Francis built still remains displaying the date stone, 1686.

*   *

Francis died in 1707 and was succeeded by his son Robert, the fourth laird (1707-1742) who was laird for thirty-five years. It must have been a sad disappointment to the family of Francis that he did not live to see "the towns and lands of Finzean erected into a Barony on 5th March 1708". No longer from this date were the titles of land and property acquired by Finzean granted by charter from the church and bishops of Aberdeen; the Farquharsons now had their own title to the land they owned. Francis Farquharson probably did much to negotiate this radical change in Finzean ownership but he was not a signatory to the final act when the Charter of Barony was granted by Queen Anne. The baronage of Scotland has always been a rank of select distinction and is still jealously retained by the thirty-seven

Scottish barons. When Robert was admitted to the baronage, there were only sixteen other barons in Scotland. While the term "baron" is not now employed and perhaps means little in twentieth century Scotland, it would certainly count for more abroad. To be introduced as the Baron of Finzean or Baron Farquharson in continental circles would immediately admit the laird to the highest society.

In 1711 Robert added the farms of Bogmore, Tillenteach and Shannel to Finzean estate. As they were the first farms to be acquired after the creation of the baronage, they were not granted by Charter from the Bishop of Aberdeen but by Charter of Adjudication under the Great Seal. Shannel and Tillenteach, the most northerly farms on the estate running down to the river Dee, have an unusual history. They had originally been granted possession to the family of Stewart in 1544 and seem to have had a special relationship with the church as the charter given that year was confirmed the following year by the Pope's Primate. About a hundred years later, during the Civil War (1657), there is a charter in the name of Oliver Cromwell evicting the Stewarts from their farms and giving the land to Thomas Spence. On the restoration of the monarchy Thomas Spence "resigned" and in 1678 the Stewarts returned to Shannel and Tillenteach and remained there until the land was acquired by the Farquharsons in 1711. But the Catholic connection continued until about 1950. A small chapel on Tillenteach with a priest's residence attached was used for worship until the early years of this century, Finzean estate receiving at that time a rent from the Roman Catholic diocese in Aberdeen. The building has now been sold and has been converted into a private residence.

Robert Farquharson was laird of Finzean at the time of the 1715 Rebellion but there seems to be no record of the Finzean Farquharsons giving support to the Jacobite cause. The Farquharsons of Invercauld and Whitehouse somewhat reluctantly supported the Earl of Mar, one of the chief leaders of the Rebellion, but Francis Farquharson of Monaltrie, the celebrated Baron Ban, showed much greater enthusiasm when at the age of 35 he led a troop of Farquharsons, somewhat depleted as many had deserted at the battle of Culloden in 1746. The Baron Ban was captured in the battle, but he survived a sentence of death and imprisonment in the Tower of London and lived on to the age of 81. Invercauld and other branches of the Farquharson clan, but not Finzean, were vassels of the Earl of Mar and had no alternative but to join the rising under his leadership, otherwise they would have been disinherited of their houses and lands. It could not have been an easy time for the Farquharsons. Their families were divided, they had difficulty in raising men to follow the Jacobite cause and they felt much was to be lost and little to be gained in supporting what many regarded as a questionable objective and forlorn hope.

During the rebellion and the years that followed, Finzean played a very low key. Not being his vassal the Finzean Farquharsons were under no obligation to follow the Earl of Mar in support of the Jacobites and there was certainly no love lost between the Farquharsons and the Gordons, their nearest Jacobite neighbours. Finzean would never have joined forces with the Gordons under the leadership of the Earl of Aboyne. The Gordons were Catholics and Robert Farquharson had been brought up a Presbyterian and was a staunch member of the Kirk of Birse where his father had been an elder for many years. It is not known whether Robert ever became an elder but he was a generous benefactor to the kirk giving in 1728 the sum of "four hundred pounds Scots to the Kirk Session for the use of the poor of the parish of Birse." There was another reason why the Farquharsons and the Gordons were not on good terms. Some years before, Francis Farquharson of Finzean had brought an action in the Court of Session against the Earl of Aboyne, claiming that the Earl's people molested the Finzean fair by preventing herdsmen from driving their cattle to be sold at the Finzean market and attempting to divert them to the Earl's mart on the other side of the Dee.

Finzean's attitude towards the Rebellion may also have been determined by the fact that Finzean had only recently been given a baronage by Queen Anne in 1707 and no doubt Robert Farquharson and his family would have regarded taking part in a rebellion against the established monarchy not only as an act of grave disloyalty to the new king but also one of gross ingratitude. The aim and purpose of the early Finzean lairds was to build up the estate and in no way did they wish to find themselves in a situation where as rebels they might risk losing the land and property they had so successfully developed for over a century.

*   *   *

Robert Farquharson died in 1742 and his son, <u>Francis</u> became the fifth laird of Finzean (1742-1786). Laird for forty-four years, Francis continued the expansion and development of the estate, at the same time managing to keep clear of the political events which had dominated Scotland during his early years as laird. As the estate grew so it became necessary for the laird to own a larger house for the comfort of his family and the entertainment of his guests. Francis added the south frontage of Finzean House on to the smaller residence built by his grandfather about fifty years before, and Finzean House was to remain in this style for the next hundred years. About this time the garden was laid out in a more formal manner and the famous holly hedge, so much a feature of Finzean garden for over two hundred years, was planted.

It was the ambition of the early Farquharson lairds to acquire all the land within the middle reaches of the valley of the River Feugh. Francis' father and grandfather had added many of the farms on the north side of the Feugh. Francis turned his attention to the south bank of the river, and in 1751 Easter and Midclune became part of the estate as well as the Forest of Glenaven, the moorland rising to the Clachnaben sky line. Ennochie, at that time the largest farm on the estate with some of the best arable land, was also acquired in 1751. Tillyfruskie was virtually the only farm within this area that continued to remain outside the bounds of the estate.

Tillyfruskie, one of the oldest properties in the parish of Birse, was first mentioned in charter in 1170. It came into the hands of the Farquharsons in 1759 having been owned and occupied by the Ochterlony family for over sixty years. Peter Ochterlony built the present "Ha' Hoose" in 1733, a charming building, typical of the period and now probably the oldest occupied building on Finzean estate. This small property might have continued in the Ochterlony family for many years had not David, the son of Peter Ochterlony, joined the army and became a great favourite of General Wolfe by whose side he was mortally wounded in the battle of Quebec in 1759.

Apart from the settlement of boundaries in the Forest of Birse fifty years later, by acquiring Tillyfruskie Francis Farquharson completed the bounds of Finzean estate within the Parish of Birse, an area of thirteen square miles or approximately 8000 acres, and so the estate was to continue for the next two hundred years.

Outside the bounds of their property in the Parish of Birse, the Farquharsons of Finzean already owned Migvie. The ambitious laird, Francis, sought to extend the property of his family even further by purchasing in 1780 a large part of Lumphanan to which he added, as he had done at Finzean, neighbouring farms as they became vacant. The property of Lumphanan included such historic sites as the Peel of Lumphanan and the hill where Macbeth was said to have been killed in 1057. Also on the Lumphanan property was the Loch of Auchinhove which was drained in 1859 by the laird and his neighbours and has since then been a most fertile area of land. In all a further 8000 acres was added by acquiring property at Migvie and Lumphanan.

Having established the boundaries of his estates at Finzean and at Lumphanan and Migvie, Francis proceeded to ensure that his lands should continue undivided for all time and that they should be held by the male heirs of the Farquharson family, provision being made for female succession in the event of the male line dying out. It was further added that the heirs on their succession had to retain the designation and arms of Farquharson of Finzean. There was provision too that the widow of a former laird should not continue to reside in Finzean House, but should receive during her lifetime one third of the rents from tenanted property. These provisions were executed in a Deed of Entail granted by the Lords of Council and Session on 27th September 1784, and they continued to apply until an Instrument of Disentail dated 19th February 1936, was executed.

With the death of Francis in 1786, there ended a period of three-quarters of a century when four lairds had succeeded their fathers, each had made a substantial contribution to the development of Finzean estate and had greatly enhanced the status of the Farquharsons of Finzean, thus to become a leading branch of the Farquharson Clan. In 1609, Robert had acquired a small area of rough land in the parish of Birse; in 1786 Francis handed on a valuable property of good farming land, most of it in the capable care of able tenants not only in Finzean itself but also in the neighbouring Farquharson property of Migvie and Lumphanan.

3. The Lean Years — 1786-1849

Francis was succeeded by his cousin, another Francis, the sixth laird (1786) who inherited the estate in his seventy-first year and survived for only nine months. He had spent most of his life in Campbeltown where he was a merchant. He probably saw little of Finzean and certainly left no mark on the estate, but he died there in 1786. He had two sons, Archibald, who became the seventh laird (1786-1796), and John, who became the ninth laird and about whom more will be written later. Archibald had closer associations with Campbeltown than with Finzean. Perhaps naturally, he was reluctant to give up a successful business in the west for the worries of an estate in the east where he had little connection. His succession to Finzean had been fairly remote and it must have come as a surprise to him. There were a few male Farquharsons who could have had prior claim to be laird of Finzean but they either died prematurely or else failed to produce male heirs. So Archibald's grandfather Donald, seeing no prospect of becoming a landed proprietor, went into business and became a merchant in Aberdeen where he sensibly married his partner's daughter, Mary Souper, who was the mother of the sixth laird, the unfortunate Francis. But Mary did not survive long and the family moved for reasons unknown to Campbeltown on the west coast where Donald successfully pursued his business and became Controller of Customs in Campbeltown. There is, however, no record to show that his control of the customs in Campbeltown was in any way related to his highly prosperous business in the town. He married again, Agnes Fleming, the daughter of a Campbeltown bailie but she died at the age of 26 leaving no children. Donald died at the age of 67 and is buried in Campbeltown beside his second wife, Agnes. Francis his son, the short-lived laird, is buried in Greyfriars Churchyard, Edinburgh, and on his tombstone there is written "Sacred to the memory of Francis Farquharson of Finzean who died 17th April, 1787 aged 70 years. And of James Farquharson, Esq. of Inverey who died at Portobello 3rd January 1817 aged 62. This stone is erected by the daughter of the former and the widow of the latter as a testimony of her great veneration and love for both."

*   *   *

Archibald Farquharson, the seventh laird (1786-1796) had spent the early years of his life in Campbeltown profitably engaged in his father's business. When he was in his fifties in 1777 he married Mary Campbell the daughter of a landowner on the island of Islay, Argyllshire but she survived only three years and left no children. She is buried in Campbeltown churchyard. After her death Archibald, a widower with few friends and little liking for the depths of the country, was obliged to spend more and more time in Finzean to which he had succeeded in 1786. According to his younger brother, John, not the most reliable source of information and for whom he had no great affection, Archibald was a very lonely man who was cared for in Finzean House by a man and two maid servants. John claims that the laird had asked the Minister of Birse to proclaim from the pulpit his proposed marriage to one of the maid servants but this the minister had refused to do. Archibald then asked another minister and a distant relative, the Rev. Robert Farquharson of Coldston in Cromar who was alleged to have read the banns but later emphatically denied having done so. So it seems no banns were read and no marriage took place.

If there was any truth in the story, it was quickly forgotten. Well into his sixties Archibald had become very friendly with Christian Spring from Aberdeen, an attractive and intelligent girl who must have been nearly forty years younger than himself. They married in 1792 when she was 25 but four years later Archibald died, leaving one son, another Archibald, the eighth laird of Finzean, who was born in 1793. The seventh laird had added little to the advancement of Finzean estate but he had one significant contribution in marrying Christian Spring. Throughout her life, and she lived to the age of 82, her interests were absorbed in the estate. She had known her husband as laird of Finzean for three years, her son as laird for 45 years and her brother-in-law, John, as laird for eight years and during this total of 56 years she had not only taken great interest in the estate but had also played an important part in its management. She had been one of the guardians of the estate, so-called "tutors", during her son's minority. The eighth laird had succeeded his father at the age of three and the estate was in the hands of tutors until he was 21. Then in the final years of her life after the death of the eighth laird, Christian assisted as best she could in the running of the estate for her aged and ailing brother-in-law, John, the absentee laird. Even more, she used to send money to the impoverished John, living in St. Albans. "Your great kindness to that helpless old man is beyond all praise," wrote her lawyer, acknowledging a gift of five pounds to John.

Christian continued to live in Finzean after her husband's death, often spending some time at 15 Pitt Street, Edinburgh which he rented. When her son, the eighth laird, sold Blackhall and took up residence in Finzean, she moved from Finzean House where she had lived for over 30 years to Auchenhove Cottage, Lumphanan, at that time within the Finzean estate, a modest house which had been built to replace the Castle of Auchenhove, destroyed by the Duke of Cumberland's forces in the '45. There she lived for 26 years until she died in 1849. She is buried in the Finzean grave in Birse churchyard.

*   *   *

Archibald Farquharson, the eighth laird (1796-1841) was born in August 1793 and a year later was baptised in Birse Kirk. On the Sunday of his baptism the kirk records note that there was a good congregation, that the collection amounted to three shillings and ninepence and that the minister preached from the text; "I cried with my whole heart; hear me, O Lord; I will keep thy statutes." There is no mention of the behaviour of young Archibald at his baptism, but the life that he was to lead gives little indication that the minister's exhortation that he should keep "the statutes of the Lord" had made any impression on the child's mind. Archibald was certainly the most colourful but also the most complex of the Finzean lairds. He became known locally as "the wild laird of Finzean" and was described by Dr Robert Farquharson, the laird one hundred years later, as "a rackety kind of person, who succeeded to a clear estate and a good lump sum of ready money, lived fast with fast people, went bankrupt and died practically of drink."

Archibald's father died when he was three years of age and he then became laird of Finzean. He was brought up by his mother, Christian, in Finzean House where he continued to live until he married. Perhaps because he was the only child of a young widowed mother, this fine looking young laird was spoilt in his youth, pampered not only by his mother but also by the servants and tenants of the estate. Educated at home by the local dominie, his upbringing had been altogether too easy. On his tenth birthday, the tenants entertained him to a sumptuous party at which a poem specially written for the occasion extolling all the virtues they expected of him, was read. One verse is sufficient to convey the tenor of the poem:

Archie Farquharson, "The Wild Laird of Finzean".

"Let virtue be his youthful choice;
True glory his chief aim;
Then if his life be short or long
He'll purchase lasting fame."

But the tenants were to become sadly disillusioned. At the age of twenty-one he married the daughter of Francis Russell of Blackhall and Glendye, neighbouring properties to Finzean. On the death of Francis Russell, the laird of Finzean acquired Blackhall and Glendye by his marriage and so Finzean commanded more property than ever before or since by adding the lands of Blackhall and Glendye to his estates of Finzean, Migvie and Lumphanan, an area totalling about 45,000 acres. For some years Archibald and his wife, Frances, enjoyed the considerable wealth of the estate, living in style and luxury. He built and occupied a splendid castle at Blackhall near Banchory where he excelled in all the sporting opportunities of fishing and shooting. He laid out a racecourse in the grounds of Blackhall and entertained lavishly the fast set of that time inviting such people as Lords Kennedy and Ross of Rossie who no doubt took full advantage of his ill advised generosity.

But there was a cloud hanging over the estate of Blackhall. During his lifetime Francis Russell, Archibald's father-in-law, had mortgaged the estate by funding road and bridge enterprises in the county, which seemed to bring no return. He had also borrowed heavily from a certain Miss Barstow, a relative of his wife, who had lived with them at Blackhall. If she was nothing else, Miss Barstow was undoubtedly a shrewd business woman who made sure that her loan would be repaid to the full at a very substantial rate of interest and that the estate would be the guarantee for her money. After Francis Russell died, Miss Barstow continued to enjoy the considerable benefit to be derived from the repayment of her loan. When Archibald succeeded to Blackhall and Glendye, he quickly realised the very heavy burden the estate was carrying and claimed that the terms of repayment to Miss Barstow were excessive and unjust. He embarked upon a costly lawsuit which he pursued through the courts to the House of Lords. After years of legal wrangle he eventually lost the case and as a result was landed not only with full repayment to Miss Barstow but also the heavy costs of the litigation.

While the case against Miss Barstow was going on, Archibald had been elected to Parliament in 1820 as a member for Elgin Burghs, and kept the seat until 1826. He showed no aptitude for politics, indeed it is doubtful whether he ever made his maiden speech, but he found plenty of time for the social life of London during the parliamentary session, at that time from January to July, then to return for the fishing and shooting on his estates and the horse racing and parties at Blackhall. Poor Archie fell further and more heavily into debt, his estates were neglected, the forests were felled, no trees were replanted and he had no alternative but to sell Blackhall and Glendye, both, it is said, at figures grossly below their value. Glendye was sold first, to Sir James Carnegie in 1823 and

Blackhall six years later to Colonel Campbell. Archie had been very reluctant to sell Blackhall as the estate so conveniently marched with Finzean and had a splendid modern mansion for his occupation. He wanted to sell Lumphanan and Migvie instead and retain Blackhall, but Finzean, Lumphanan and Migvie had all been entailed by Archibald Farquharson, the seventh laird, in 1790, and the entail could only be broken by an Act of Parliament. As he was a member of Parliament at the time Archie attempted to do this but he got little or no support for his efforts. So Blackhall was sold and the great estate of 45,000 acres was reduced again to 16,000 acres first by the sale of Glendye and later by that of Blackhall after a period of only 15 years.

About the same time (1812) Archie was involved in another costly civil case with the Earl of Aboyne when the division of the Forest of Birse Commonty was disputed between the two claimants. The whole question of rights of Commonty proved to be a lawyers' paradise and the case continued for many months at the end of which Finzean seemed to be the loser, retaining only the small farm of Auchabrack from a large area of moorland and a much smaller area of arable land.

Although Archibald made no mark in Westminster he was remembered for many years in his constituency as having been a leading party in the notorious "Raid of Elgin". Lord Seafield and his family, particularly his three beautiful daughters, were strong political supporters of Archibald in his election campaign for Elgin Burghs, while the Earl of Fife and his family supported his opponent, General Alexander Duff. During the 1820 election feeling ran very high; there had been bribery and kidnapping, even the beautiful Seafield daughters were mobbed in the streets of Elgin. The climax came when the supporters of General Duff kidnapped a prominent Elgin councillor, shipping him across the Moray Firth to Sutherland. There were even ugly rumours that a similar fate was to befall the Seafield daughters. Greatly alarmed, the Earl of Seafield sent a messenger to Strathspey to summon his clansmen and Archibald was instructed to seek such help as he could muster. The messenger reached Cromdale on a Sunday morning as the congregation was coming out of church and about three hundred men immediately set off for Elgin. By Monday morning over seven hundred supporters of Seafield and Archie Farquharson stood guard outside Grant Lodge, the home of the three terrified daughters. Meantime the adherents of the Earl of

Fife were pouring in from the fishing villages armed with a variety of obsolete weapons, and it seemed that a serious breach of the peace was imminent. The sheriff of the county was summoned and arrived in a great state. Whether it was due to his intervention or to the good sense of the people of Elgin is not known, but the situation in the town quietened down. For several days special constables paraded the streets and the people were warned to light their windows to save them from being broken. After the election which resulted in the return of Archibald Farquharson, the town of Elgin soon assumed its normal life, but for many years "the Raid of Elgin" was remembered.

But in Edinburgh the affair at Elgin was quickly forgotten. Two years later in 1822 Archibald Farquharson was chosen to be one of the household at the Palace of Holyrood House to attend on George IV during his celebrated state visit to Scotland.

Archibald did not stand for re-election to Parliament in 1826. From then until his death in 1841 he and his wife Frances spent most of their time in Finzean contributing little to the improvement of the estate. What was left of a substantial fortune at one time was now considerably depleted. The extravagent parties of earlier years were continued on a more modest scale but there were stories of wagers that were taken for all sorts of challenges, one of which was to see who could crawl furthest along the top of the massive holly hedge surrounding the garden of Finzean House. Sometimes their parties were held in local inns and there is amongst the papers of Archie's lawyer at that time, an unpaid bill from the Charlestown Inn, Aboyne, amounting to two pounds and sixpence for food ("eating"), wine, whisky punch, porter and beer, and hay and corn for eight horses. Presumably Archie and his friends had ridden over from Finzean to enjoy a night out.

Archie was probably drinking heavily in his latter years. At the age of 47, a year before his death, he was involved in a childish case, unbecoming to a laird of Finzean. He came before the sheriff at Stonehaven and was fined £10 for mixing a purgative with a pound of tea which he had presented to the members of "the total abstinence society" for their soiree at Banchory and sending with it a note "from a well wisher to the health and prosperity of the society". No doubt the society had tried unsuccessfully to persuade Archie to mend his ways.

There is a portrait by Sir Henry Raeburn of Archie Farquharson in the Aberdeen Art Gallery, probably painted shortly before he became a Member of Parliament when he was about 25 years of age. He is shown as a casually tailored gentleman of his time, tall dark and handsome with strikingly dark brown eyes and sensuous lips: as one would expect of the work of such a great painter as Raeburn, a likeness depicting the true character of the man.

Archie died at Finzean on 14th May, 1841, at the age of 47, and was buried in Birse Churchyard where there is a memorial over the grave erected by his wife, Frances, which is dedicated as "a tribute to that unbroken conjugal affection which subsisted between them for 26 years".

*   *   *

Archie and Frances had no children so succession to Finzean stepped back one generation to Archie's uncle, John, the ninth laird (1841-1849). John was probably in his early sixties when he inherited the property. He knew little and cared less about the estate, and if he visited it at all, it must have been very infrequently during the lifetime of his brother Archibald, the seventh laird. It is unlikely that he would have been the guest of his nephew with whom he was not on good terms. John spent much of his life abroad or latterly at St. Albans where he became hopelessly under the influence of an unscrupulous lawyer, William Scott, who had previously ruined his family in banking speculation. Scott had an eye on the opportunities he could gain if and when John inherited Finzean and it is no doubt because of this that John was forced to take a strong line in opposing Archie's proposal to disentail Lumphanan and Migvie. Had the estates been disentailed and sold, Archie would probably have gone through another fortune and John, to say nothing of William Scott, would have been left without any prospect of a substantial means of support.

The estate's lawyers in Scotland (William Fraser, WS and James Hagart of Edinburgh, and Robert Smith, advocate in Aberdeen) became extremely suspicious of the manoeuvres of William Scott. Added to John's opposition to the disentail of the estate, Fraser was greatly alarmed to hear a rumour in 1844 that old John was to get married, clearly with the hope that Finzean would be kept for his immediate family and for the continued benefit of Scott. Hagart, who represented others interested in the family succession, was enraged and wrote to Smith "If the old blockhead is resolved to act the fool and blackguard, as William Fraser suspects, I very much fear that nothing anyone can say or do can prevent him . . . you should represent the prospects of any widow the old idiot may leave in as unfavourable a light as truth will permit . . ."

For some time the anxiety continued. The lawyers made a long journey to St. Albans several times in order to see John but the door was closed in their faces. When Dr. Graham, a friend of the family, was refused entrance to the house, he appealed to the mayor of St. Albans as a magistrate but this approach did not seem to have been successful. In a letter to one of the lawyers, Dr. Graham wrote "to me it is perfectly clear that Mr. Farquharson is a prisoner and is not allowed the slightest excuse of his own free will — but great pains are taken to amuse and cajole him."

As time passed it became fairly certain that John would not marry and that this unhappy line of the Farquharson clan would shortly end. The Scottish lawyers decided to let the matter rest if only to safeguard the remote succession to Finzean that was to follow. Their fears were at an end with the death of Scott in 1847. His son Charles continued to handle John's affairs but with much less persistence. John was shortly released from his St. Albans' captivity, went north to Edinburgh and died there in 1849.

In his will, John left various small bequests but nothing to Charles Scott. Some money was left to Bishop Gillis for the building of a new cathedral, to Roman Catholic schools in Edinburgh, to the next laird, Dr. Francis Farquharson, "my watch, chain and seals with the arms of Finzean" and the residue to a certain Mary Lucy Fraser "as a token of my affection towards her". Was she the bride that never was?

III

The Family of Francis Farquharson 1802-1876 (10th Laird of Finzean) and m. (a) Alison Mary Ainslie d. 1863,
(b) Mary Anne Girdwood 1838-1914

William
1833-1866

Robert
1836-1918
(11th Laird of Finzean)

Francis
1842
d. inf.

John
1843-1859

Joseph
1846-1935
m. 1914 Violet
Evelyn Jay
(12th Laird of Finzean)

James
1850-1918

4. The Recovery of Finzean

After John's death in 1849, succession to Finzean was remote, but nevertheless was not unexpected by the tenth laird Francis Farquharson (1849-1876). Francis was a very distant cousin of John. In order to establish Francis' right to be laird of Finzean, inheritance had to be traced back to the second laird, Alexander, in the seventeenth century. The elder son of Alexander had inherited Finzean, but the senior branch of the family ended with the death of John. It was through the junior branch of Alexander's family that Francis became laird. The junior branch of the Farquharsons had for three generations been lairds at Balfour, a nearby estate on Deeside, but in 1790 Balfour was sold to the Marquis of Huntly and then some years later to Francis Cochran, an advocate in Aberdeen, whose firm continues to be the factors of Finzean Estate to the present day.

Francis Farquharson was born in 1802, the son of William Farquharson, a distinguished Edinburgh doctor who became President of the Royal College of Surgeons. Francis followed in his father's footsteps, graduated in medicine at Edinburgh University and set up his practice in the new town of Edinburgh. Although he was a busy man working long hours, his practice was not regarded as being very lucrative. But for a young man time could always be found for relaxation and there was much to attract his attention by becoming very friendly with the Ainslie family who lived conveniently near his home in Northumberland Street and who had several beautiful and eligible daughters. Alison Mary Ainslie was a celebrated beauty in Edinburgh society and after months of competitive wooing it was she who was to become the wife of Francis Farquharson of Finzean.

His father, Robert Ainslie, was a much respected Writer to the Signet in Edinburgh and had in his earlier years been a close friend of Robert Burns. They had toured the borders of Scotland together and so greatly enjoyed one another's company that on his return to Edinburgh, Robert Burns wrote to Ainslie on 23rd November 1787:

> "You will think it romantic when I tell you that I find the idea of your friendship almost necessary to my existence. You assume a proper length of face in my bitter hours of devildom and you laugh fully up to my highest wishes at my good things. I doubt, upon the whole, if you are one of the best fellows in God's World, but you are so to me."

Francis Farquharson, the tenth laird.

But it was not just to his travelling companion that Burns showed his regard. At the end of their Border tour, they stopped off at Berrywell, near Duns, the home of Robert Ainslie's father and there Burns met Rachel Ainslie, Robert's sister and Alison Mary's aunt. On the Sunday they all went to church at Duns and were given a lengthy discourse by Dr. Bowmaker denouncing the evils of obstinate sin. During the sermon Burns observed Rachel turning over the leaves of her Bible searching for the text upon which the denunciation was based. He took out a piece of paper, wrote the following lines on it and slipped it along the pew:

"Fair maid, you need not take the hint, or idle text pursue
'Twas guilty sinners that he meant, not angels such as you."

The next day Robert Ainslie returned to Edinburgh leaving Robert Burns and Rachel together with his ageing parents. The flirtation developed; it is unlikely Burns had matrimonial intentions but he was inspired to write lines of affection in his diary:

"Found Miss Ainslie all alone at Berrymore. Heavenly powers who know the weakness of human hearts support mine. What happiness must I see only to remind me that I cannot enjoy it. How well looking, how frank, how good she is! Charming Rachel, may thy bosom never be wrung by the evils of this life of sorrow, or the villainy of this world's sons."

Two of Burns' letters to Alison Mary's father were kept by the lairds of Finzean until they were destroyed in a disastrous fire in Finzean House in 1954.

*   *   *

Francis and Alison Mary were married in Edinburgh in 1832 and quickly settled down in Northumberland Street. Within the year William was born, to be followed by five more sons, all within a period of seventeen years.

William, the eldest, was born in 1833, served with the 92nd Highlanders, fought in the Crimean War and died unmarried in 1866.

Robert was born in 1836, succeeded his father as laird of Finzean in 1876 and died in 1918.

Francis was born about 1842 and died in infancy.

John was born in 1843 and died in 1859 at the age of 16 as the result of an accident while at school at Glenalmond. There is a fine memorial window to John in the school chapel and also a single cross at the back of Finzean House inscribed with the letters J.F.

Joseph was born in 1846, married Violet Hay of Blackhall in 1914, succeeded his brother Robert as laird of Finzean in 1918 and died without issue in 1935.

James was born about 1850. Little is known about him except that he died at Romsey unmarried in 1918.

In many respects they were a remarkable family, but in one respect they were unique; six sons but no direct heirs from the family.

Edinburgh has often had the reputation of attaching undue importance to social division, but never more so than in the nineteenth century in the education of her sons. In the New Town this distinction was evident as one proceeded from Princes Street northwards beyond the Queen Street Gardens. Boys from the prestigious Heriot Row would usually be educated privately or sent to expensive boarding schools. Boys from Great King Street and Northumberland Street would probably go as day boys to the nearby Edinburgh Academy but further north into Cumberland Street and Fettes Row, boys would have to make do with the more rugged and basic education of the local burgh school.

The Farquharson boys came within the middle band and five of them went to the Edinburgh Academy. John spent four years at the Academy before going on to Glenalmond; Joseph left the Academy early in order to develop his artistic talents at the Board of Manufacture School, Edinburgh. The Academy, only twenty years old when the eldest son, William, became a pupil in 1843, had been established to provide a sound classical education for the boys of the New Town of Edinburgh and throughout its long history it has continued to teach many boys who can claim Farquharson connections.

*   *   *

With a growing family and an increasing practice, the Farquharsons moved from Northumberland Street to a larger house at 5 Eton Terrace. They had not been there many years before Francis became laird of Finzean. He gave up his practice and moved to Finzean with his family although they kept on the house in Edinburgh for some years to provide a base for the education of the boys. Robert recalls their arrival at Finzean.

"I remember the shock we received when we first saw Finzean. It was a veritable barn, old without being venerable, and although built nearly two hundred years ago, it had none of the charms of antiquity. It looked dull, dreary, common and depressing; it was surrounded by a big holly hedge and all around was a bare, neglected garden. The furniture was of the most meagre kind, as might have been expected from a place in the hands of a bankrupt and subsequent trustees.

However, the estate had assets; there was some fine timber still standing, the agricultural land was tenanted and had above average fertility although the farm houses and steadings had been sadly neglected and were in poor shape; the sporting facilities were excellent with a good grouse moor, pheasant and partridge shooting in the valley and over at Lumphanan, and a fine stretch of the river Dee for good salmon fishing.

On his arrival at Finzean in 1849 Francis began immediately to improve his estates but as a result of his efforts four years later he was already in debt to the tune of over £4500, a sum which had to be met by granting bonds against the estate. Because the estate was entailed, the granting of a bond could only be sanctioned by approval of the Court of Session in Edinburgh, a costly and often lengthy legal procedure. But it all proved to be well worthwhile. Finzean House which was out of date and quite inadequate for his large family was modernised to the standards of the time and a beautiful garden was laid out around the house within the historic holly hedge. The estate policies were planned with carriage roads in and around the replanted woodlands, eventually to produce some of the tallest and finest Scots fir in Scotland and to become known as the Lairds' Walking Sticks. But it was probably on the agricultural side that Francis Farquharson made his great contribution to his estates at Finzean and Lumphanan. He spent large sums of money in draining the fields and so increasing their productivity. Dykes and later fences were built to divide up the land into convenient and economic farm units. And to each farm he ensured there was a suitable steading and habitable farm house. This was a process which took many years to carry out; indeed the work started in 1849 was still continuing into the early years of the twentieth century. Familiar names of Finzean tenants began to appear in the estate records of the late eighteenth and early nineteenth centuries. A certain John Low was granted the tenancy of the Finzean farm of Easter Clune in 1764 and within the next half century leases were granted to Anderson of Tillygarmond, Mortimer of Clinter and Thow of Ennochie, all families continuing to farm Finzean land to the present day.

With the improvements to his estate and an increase in its population, so its life developed. Francis built the church at Finzean in 1863. The estate of Finzean is in the parish of Birse and up to that time the people of Finzean used to attend the church at Birse, a distance of some six miles from the centre of the estate. On many a Sunday it must have been a cold and uncomfortable journey walking or driving over the hill of Corsedarder to Birse church but in summer or winter the attendance from Finzean was good. Francis did a great service to the people by providing them with a church near at hand in the centre of the estate. There are memorials to Francis and his first wife in the church as well as memorials to other members of the Farquharson family. In other respects the needs of the estate were provided. There were blacksmiths and tailors and shoemakers and an active social life on the estate. A feature of the new home farm steading at Finzean was a large hall where there were dinners, dances, and dramatic entertainments, and people used to come from far and wide to hear two celebrated local fiddlers, Brown of the Bucket Mill and Mortimer of Clinter. The garden parties at Finzean House gave the tenants and their families the opportunity not only to meet the laird and his family but also to see the improvements to "the big hoos" and the attractions of the new garden with its spacious lawns and flower beds all within the historic holly hedge.

*　　　*　　　*

Francis was a dedicated and popular laird and in both his marriages he was supported by wives who were devoted to Finzean. Alison Mary, his first wife, brought up a family of six boys while at the same time playing an important role as hostess in Edinburgh and in Finzean during the early years of its development. She was much more than a woman of great beauty, she had literary and artistic talents, which he handed down to her sons. She had a gracious quality of life acquired in the society of Edinburgh which she brought to Finzean and Deeside. She died in 1863 and is buried in Birse churchyard.

Twelve months later, almost to the day, Francis at the age of 62 married again, a bride thirty-six years younger than himself. She was Mary Ann Girdwood, the second daughter of Thomas Girdwood of Newington, Edinburgh, a family of considerable wealth. In twelve years they lived happily at Finzean House, seldom moving away from the estate, and in 1876 when Francis died Mary Anne was left to look after her step-family which she continued to do with great devotion until 1914 when she died at the age of seventy-six. She had been mistress of Finzean House for fifty years, twelve years with her husband and 38 years as a widow looking after "the boys" if such they could be called as Robert was 78 and Joseph was 68 when their step-mother died. They had been devoted to her and it was said that because she became so completely a part of their lives they had no cause to seek the attentions of anyone else, remaining bachelors during her lifetime. However, only a few months after Mary Anne died, Joseph at the age of 68 married Violet Hay of Blackhall, Banchory, who was only 27.

*　　　*　　　*

Francis was a remarkable man of great energy, short in stature but with strong physique having, it was said at the time, the second largest head in Edinburgh. On his large head he frequently wore an outsize grey top hat which gave him the appearance of being top heavy. In his large head there were many talents. His first real talent was art which he might have followed as a career had he not been discouraged by his father, Dr. William Farquharson. Somewhat reluctantly he followed in his father's footsteps and became a doctor, a general practitioner in Edinburgh, but attaining some eminence as an oculist. When he inherited Finzean in 1849, he gave up his practice and devoted his whole life to the estates. It was said that after coming to Finzean he would not even see local people who complained of some illness. To one tenant seeking medical advice he said "the skill of my doctoring's a' awa'." At first coming from Edinburgh he had little knowledge of rural matters but he quickly set

Francis Farquharson with his second wife Mary Anne Girdwood, and William and Joseph.

to and with great determination and by good management he improved the land and the standards of the people. Both at Finzean and Lumphanan he had long-term plans for the development of agriculture and forestry and when he died after 27 years as laird his hopes were beginning to be realised. Finzean owes a great debt of gratitude to Francis Farquharson who undoubtedly contributed more to the development of the estate than any earlier laird.

Francis died in 1876 at the age of 74 and is buried in the family graveyard at Birse beside his first wife, Alison Mary Ainslie. There is also a memorial to Francis in the Dean Cemetery in Edinburgh at the grave of his second wife, Mary Anne Girdwood, and nearby are the graves of his eldest son, William, and his fourth son, John. The Dean Cemetery is within a half a mile of Eton Terrace where Francis had brought up his family in Edinburgh and in the neighbourhood where he worked as a family doctor in his earlier years.

Robert Farquharson, M.P., the eleventh laird.

5. Robert, MP and Joseph, RA

Robert, ("Cousin Bob"), the eleventh laird (1876-1918), was 40 when he succeeded to Finzean on the death of his father. He was born in Northumberland Street, Edinburgh and at the age of ten went to the Edinburgh Academy. Unlike a classmate at the Academy, James Clark Maxwell, the pioneer of wireless telegraphy, who was reading mathemetical papers to the Royal Society of Edinburgh at the age of 15, Robert achieved no great distinction at school but he had sufficient learning to pass the tests required in those days for entry to Edinburgh University where he graduated in medicine, later being awarded a Doctorate of Medicine at the age of 32. Unfortunately for Robert the family practice in Edinburgh had been sold when his father went to Finzean and the family fortunes at that time being at such a low ebb that there was not the means to set him up in another practice. So Robert sought a career as a doctor in the army and he soon received a commission, first in the Royal Artillery and later in the Coldstream Guards. As an army doctor, life was to his liking; it was not too strenuous and he enjoyed the convivial friendship of the officers' mess. He had no service abroad, most of his time being spent in London where he enthusiastically entered into the life of London society.

After nine years in the army he resigned his commission and became medical officer to Rugby School where he enjoyed the company of the masters' common room although he stood in awe of the head master, the great Dr. Temple. But the income of a school doctor was very variable and sometimes minimal as at that time it depended upon fees paid by the parents of boys who fell ill. He hopefully attended every Rugby football match and was always first on the field when there was an injury to be attended to. He frankly admitted that his best term for financial reward happened when an epidemic of German measles attacked the school. Work at Rugby suited him well and he was able to visit Finzean more frequently. During the long summer holidays he shot grouse on the Finzean moors and of course Rugby was not too far distant from London to allow him to continue his social engagements.

At Rugby Robert must have realised that he was not making the most of his medical knowledge. His next move was back to London where he seriously settled down to hard work. While practising in general medicine, he studied and was admitted a Fellow of the Royal College of Physicians, eventually becoming a lecturer at St. Mary's Hospital, London. It was in the science of pharmacology, and particularly in its application to children, that he was to gain a considerable reputation, and on the strength of his work in this field he was appointed consultant physician to the Belgrave Hospital for Children, his last medical appointment.

A year after he succeeded to Finzean Robert gave up medicine and for a few years devoted all his interests to continuing the good work on the estate which his father had started. No doubt he yearned for a fuller life than Finzean could offer at that time. He had always been interested in politics, his father having been an ardent Radical, and at Rugby he came under the influence of Dr Temple, a leading Radical thinker of his time. So Robert embarked upon a political career and sat as Liberal Member of Parliament for West Aberdeenshire continuously for 26 years from 1880 to 1906. He fought six elections and despite keen Conservative opposition was successful on every occasion. He was a moderate Liberal, a Gladstonian, who faithfully followed the party whip through the division lobbies. For half his membership in the House of Commons, Mr. Gladstone was leader of the Liberal Party and Prime Minister but Gladstone stood aloof and Robert did not get to know him well. Robert's ambitions in Parliament were limited but at one time there was talk of him being offered a junior ministerial post which might have led to higher office. Robert tells of an occasion at a time when there was a cabinet re-shuffle when he thought his hopes were to be realised. Unexpectedly one evening after a division in the House, he was summoned to the Prime Minister's room. Ushered in, he stood in front of the great man wondering what post he had to offer and whether he should accept it immediately. The Prime Minister quickly looked up from his papers, blurted out "I liked your brother's picture in this year's Royal Academy. Good-bye." No more was said and no offer was ever made.

When Sir Henry Campbell-Bannerman succeeded Mr Gladstone as leader of the party, relationships were entirely different. Sir Henry was a personal friend of Robert and often visited him at Finzean, but by the time Campbell-Bannerman became leader, the Liberals were in opposition and there was no opportunity of office for Robert. However, in 1906 when Robert retired from Parliament he was made a Privy Councillor, in recognition of his political services and also probably because Finzean was conveniently near Balmoral so that Robert could easily attend Privy Council meetings during the King's stay in Scotland. There is an interesting footnote to Robert's political ambitions. During the Constitutional Crisis of 1911 when the King was to be asked to create a sufficient number of Liberal peers to ensure the passage though the Lords of the governments' measure to limit the powers of the House of Lords, a list of names of suitable persons for elevation to the peerage was prepared and held in strictest secrecy. The list was found in Mr Asquith's papers after his death and the third name on the list was that of the Right Honourable Robert Farquharson, PC, MD, LL D.

Robert's Liberal views frequently did not endear him to his fellow lairds. His party supported measures which favoured the tenant rather than the landlord and Robert faithfully followed the party line. He spoke frequently on agricultural matters, particularly as they affected Scotland, and he was disappointed when he was not called to deliver a well-prepared maiden speech on an agricultural bill giving farmers for the first time compensation for inexhausted improvements. He was to meet more criticism from his fellow lairds when he proposed an amendment to a Grouse Game Bill which intended to enable a farmer to protect himself from the ravages of grouse on fields adjacent to the moors. At the same time, as if it had been painted in support of his brother, Joseph had a picture hung in the Royal Academy entitled *Highland Raiders* depicting damage being done by coveys of grouse on a stooked cornfield. But Robert's amendment was unsuccessful. What aroused the anger of the Aberdeenshire lairds more than anything else was Robert's failure to support the Conservative government in its conduct of the Boer War. On a vote of confidence in the government in 1900, the Liberals were divided; one-third voted with the government, one-third against and one-third abstained. Robert followed his friend and party leader, Campbell-Bannerman, and abstained. He also spoke on medical matters, and from his short experience in the army, he felt he was entitled to speak at the annual debate on the army estimates.

While Robert made no major contribution as a member of Parliament, he was a hardworking and very popular figure in the House of Commons. He attended diligently and if he was not to be seen as frequently in the chamber of the House, "the Doctor", as he was affectionately called, would certainly be found in the smoking room. When he retired in 1906, Campbell-Bannerman wrote of him, "His genial temperament, his courteous and kindly demeanour, his cheerful spirit, his keen interest in all public affairs which was guided by a good share of national commonsense — these good qualities attracted the affection of us all."

During the long parliamentary vacations, Robert spent much of his time at Finzean attending to estate matters with his brother, Joseph. Although Joseph was ten years younger than Robert, they managed the estate as a partnership. They were both devoted to

Finzean but neither of them contributed so much to the improvement of the estate as their father had done before them. Works which Francis had started were continued or completed and standards were maintained and further alterations and improvements were made to Finzean House by the addition of more bathrooms and two large picture windows, a feature of each side of the house. The two brothers and their step-mother moved around the estate in a benevolent manner knowing everyone by name and being greeted with respect and affection. The tenants and the estate workers were proud of their lairds and rejoiced in their successes. While Robert was a Member of Parliament and Joseph was a Royal Academician, for much of the year there was great activity at Finzean House. Their step-mother was their able and charming hostess both in London and at Finzean assisted by a staff who travelled to and fro every year. At Finzean there were regular lunch parties, often very democratic in character, with the nobility sitting down beside the schoolmaster and the older tenants. My grandfather, John Marshall Lang, then Principal of Aberdeen University, was often at Finzean House and there met among others Lord Aberdeen, Sir Henry Campbell-Bannerman and Harry Lauder. There were shooting parties on the hill, the start often delayed while the Doctor related at length the latest stories from London, much to the annoyance and impatience of his brother, Joseph, who was anxious to get on with the shoot. There were dramatic entertainments in the hall at the home farm and tenants' dinners to celebrate any worthwhile occasion. On one such occasion in 1909 the laird entertained his tenants to a five course dinner after which thirteen toasts were proposed. And every year before his return to London, the laird would visit the village school with books for the senior pupils and sweets for all.

This very humane laird with considerable talents and a wide variety of interests but at times eccentric in behaviour was an invalid during the latter years of his life, spending his time in the beautiful garden at Finzean House and on his beloved estate. Robert died early in 1918 and is buried in Birse Churchyard.

*   *   *

1914 was a year of change in Finzean House. In March, Mary Anne, the second wife of Francis and step-mother to Robert and Joseph, died at the age of 76. Married at 26 she became a widow 12 years later and for the remaining 38 years of her life she graciously devoted herself to looking after her step-sons and to the people of the estate. Six months later, in September of 1914, almost as if he had been waiting the opportunity, Joseph at the age of 68 married Violet Hay of Blackhall who was 27. Blackhall was a neighbouring estate to Finzean and had for a short time been Farquharson property before it was sold by Archie Farquharson in 1829. And in August 1914, the Great War broke out. Although the war had little immediate impact on the estate, social activities virtually ended and gradually the younger generation of estate and farm workers were called to the forces. In many ways too, 1914 began the decline of an era of territorial artistocracy in rural areas and in this respect Finzean was no exception.

*   *   *

Joseph (Cousin Joe) became the twelfth laird of Finzean (1918-1935), when his brother Robert died in 1918. Although he was born in Edinburgh in 1846 and like his brothers had been educated at the

Joseph Farquharson, R.A., the twelfth laird.

Edinburgh Academy, he spent most of his life at Finzean. From his earliest years Joseph developed an outstanding talent for painting inherited partly from his father who was a born painter and partly from his mother's family, the Ainslies, from whom he derived an intuitive and sensitive appreciation of pastoral scenes which inspired much of his work. His father, Francis, had a small studio in his Edinburgh house and during the weekend, Joseph was allowed the use of the studio. It was from there and while he was still only fifteen that he had his first picture hung in the Royal Scottish Academy under the title given in the catalogue *Study from Nature*. After he left school, Joseph studied art at the Board of Manufacture School, Edinburgh, the unattractive title given at the time to a college which eventually became the Edinburgh College of Art. He also attended the life school of the Royal Scottish Academy. Later he went on to Paris to study painting under Carolus Duran and side by side with the celebrated portrait painter, John S. Sargent. Joseph quickly found a place in artistic society and was recognised not only for his talents but also for his genial personality. He lived at a time when the influence of the great paintings of the French Impressionists must have inspired his work. He was after all a contemporary of the later Impressionists, of Monet and of Renoir, and he may indeed have met them in the artistic salons of Paris although there is no record of this.

His earlier exhibits in the Royal Scottish Academy showed greater versatility than his later work when he concentrated more on the winter pastoral scene for which he was to become famous. He exhibited portraits and a series of pictures of street scenes in Egypt which he visited for several years with a group of fellow painters. Inevitably there were pictures with a moral for which Victorian painters have such a passion. Later in life he painted some of his best pictures in the West Highlands of Scotland from a house he had bought at Loch Linnhe but as Violet, his wife, was never happy away from Finzean, his visits to the west coast became more and more infrequent. Within six months of his death, Violet sold Coruanan, their house on the west coast.

After his first acceptance in 1861, Joseph Farquharson continued to exhibit annually at the Royal Scottish Academy and in 1873 he had his first picture hung in the Royal Academy in London. Surprisingly he was never a Royal Scottish Academician, his taking up residence in London about 1877 debarring him from election to the Scottish Academy, but in 1915 he was awarded the highest accolade of the

English art establishment by becoming a Royal Academician.

From 1861 to 1935 he exhibited continuously either at the Royal Scottish Academy or the Royal Academy in London, the only break in a span of 74 years being 1914, the year of his marriage. There is no record of the total number of pictures painted by Joseph Farquharson but catalogues show that he had 290 pictures exhibited in the two Royal Academies and there were certainly many more in other galleries and private collections. Some years after his death a collection of his pictures, some unfinished, were found in his studio in Finzean and many of them fetched a considerable sum for the benefit of his widow.

For most of his painting life his work was devoted to winter scenes in Scotland and mainly around Finzean. He seemed to prefer painting the softer colours of evening light with woodland scenes, snow, sunsets and, of course, sheep. He described himself as a commercial artist and it was certainly true that he painted for a living, and at times very profitably. At the height of his career his pictures fetched high prices and there was also much to be made from the sale of signed prints which still adorn many houses throughout Scotland. Latterly Farquharson paintings became popular subjects for illustrated calenders and Christmas cards.

Finzean was never a wealthy estate and an income had to be found from one source or another. The sale of his pictures proved to be sufficiently profitable not only to make provision for the Finzean household and the estate but also to assist Robert Farquharson's career in politics and their life in London. The Farquharsons could live comfortably, if not lavishly, at Finzean and in London, but when the income from art began to drop, the Farquharson household had to tighten its belt. When Joseph died in 1935, he left sufficient provision for his widow to allow her to spend the remaining years of her life at Finzean in modest circumstances, but so long as she was allowed to live in Finzean that was all she wanted.

Joseph did not only paint when the spirit moved him; he was a hard-working artist, rising early to be at his studio by nine thirty and continuing until sunset with a break for gin and lunch. His admirers have often wondered how he managed to paint so realistically scenes of bitter cold weather. The answer was that he had a caravan with a large window, comfortably furnished and heated with an anthracite stove, and from there he would make sketches for the paintings to be completed in a spacious studio in the home farm steading.

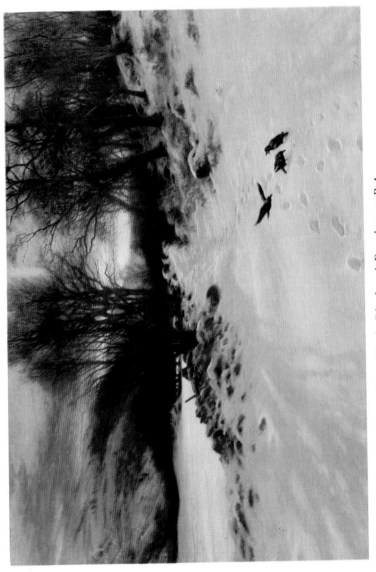

"A Winter Morning" by Joseph Farquharson, R.A.
(By permission of the Manchester City Art Gallery).

His pictures were certainly numerous and varied in quality. Some have become recognised as works achieving the highest standards of landscape painting; others, he would be the first to admit, had less artisitic merit. But Joseph Farquharson will be remembered as a distinguished interpreter of the Scottish scene and one who has contributed many beautiful works to the Scottish school of painting.

*   *   *

For nearly sixty years Robert and Joseph were lairds of Finzean and were resident on the estate for much of the time. It was not in their nature to concern themselves too closely with the affairs of the estate. Their legal and financial interests were looked after by the estate factors in Aberdeen while the resident ground officers both at Finzean and Lumphanan took care of the detail as instructed by the factors. At that time a laird was not expected to worry about the requirements of his tenants; he had an overall interest in their welfare but so far as the terms of a tenancy were concerned, such problems as were brought to their notice would be quickly passed on to the factor. The rents at Finzean were low and correspondingly the tenants' requirements were few.

They were both popular and kindly lairds, always ready to stop and talk to the tenantry, to make frequent visits to the thriving school and to interest themselves in the social activities of the estate. Although neither of them was a pillar of the kirk, nevertheless Robert had been largely responsible for building Finzean manse in 1902 as his father 40 years before had built the church. In 1928 Joseph presented the estate with a spacious village hall to which further facilities were added by the community at a later date.

Both Robert and Joseph were keen sportsmen, Joseph having the reputation of being one of the finest shots on Deeside. One year on the twelfth of August when nearly 200 brace of grouse were shot on the Finzean moor, 90 brace fell to Joseph's gun. They had less enthusiasm for fishing; Robert seldom fished and Joseph only occasionally so the valuable stretch on the River Dee, the Commonty, was normally let to fishing tenants. The salmon fishing rights of the Commonty had been shared for over a hundred years between Finzean and the neighbouring estate of Ballogie, apart from a short stretch which belonged outright to Finzean. Towards the end of 1930 the Crown, having property adjacent to the Commonty, disputed the rights of Finzean and Ballogie and claimed an exclusive right to the salmon fishing on the Commonty. Joseph Farquharson with Colonel Randall Nicol of Ballogie challenged the claims of the Crown and a protracted law suit followed in the Court of Session in Edinburgh. Joseph Farquharson, now over 85, gave evidence as a witness and the whole case caused him great anxiety. Evidence was produced dating back to the sixteenth century, presenting the Court with a volume of documents (of which the Barony Charter to Finzean of 1708 was the most important), and witnesses from poachers to proprietors appeared in the witness box. Eventually the court decided in favour of Finzean and Ballogie; the Crown did not appeal to the House of Lords, and expenses, which were considerable, were awarded in favour of the two estates. This was an important day for Finzean — to confirm, as had so often been claimed, that it was one of the finest estates of its size in Aberdeenshire, with agricultural land, forestry, a grouse moor and salmon fishing, and an estate manor in an unrivalled situation.

The strain of the Commonty fishing case over, Joseph relapsed into a decline and for the last three years of his life he was a complete invalid enjoying only the beauty of the garden he had created and the loving care of his wife, Violet. Joseph died at Finzean in May 1935 in his eighty-ninth year and was buried in the family burial ground at Birse. He was the last of the six sons of Francis, the only one to be married but leaving no direct heir to suceed at Finzean estate.

*   *   *

At the age of 68 Joseph had married Violet Hay, a bride 41 years younger than himself. Perhaps it was surprising that Joseph, knowing that he was the only one of his brothers who was likely to provide an heir to the estate, did not marry when he was a younger man. He was certainly a most eligible bachelor, handsome, talented, and with prospects of landed inheritance in Scotland, a young man who must have attracted the attention of women in artistic and society circles and on his travels in the continent and the Middle East.

His life as a young man had not been without romance, but a romance which was never allowed to lead to marriage. His father, Francis Farquharson, and his family had always been very close to the family of Joseph Cauvin Farquharson, his younger brother. The two families had lived nearby in Edinburgh before Francis inherited Finzean, the boys had been at school together and there must have been many comings and goings between the households during the gracious social life of Edinburgh of the mid-Victorian era. In the winter there would have been family parties for birthdays and Christmas in the elegant gas-lit drawing rooms of Eton Terrace and Inverleith Place, with charades for the children and singing and dancing for the adults, with faithful family retainers to attend on them. During the summer the families would venture out for family picnics in their horse-drawn carriages, as far afield as the Pentland Hills or the shores of South Queensferry.

Of this generation of the children of Francis and Joseph Cauvin, boys were very much in the majority, there being nine boys to only two girls, both daughters of Joseph Cauvin. Madeline was the youngest of the girls, very beautiful, lively and attractive and only six years younger than her cousin, Joe. When she was not yet eighteen Madeline and Joe fell in love and despite considerable difficulties the romance developed. But the course of true love was not to run smoothly. Both Madeline's parents had died before she was sixteen and she desperately needed the advice they would have given her. At the age of twenty she was left to look after the two orphan sons of her brother David and his wife, Julia, who had both died an early age. But the fact that Madeline and Joe were cousins forbad any proposal of marriage. It must have been a confusing situation for poor Madeline without the comfort and advice of her father and mother or of her eldest sister and brother who by that time had gone abroad. Joe's father and his stepmother, Mary Anne Girdwood, positively forbad the marriage. By now Francis was getting an old man; Mary Anne was young and beautiful and only eight years older than Joe. One cannot help wondering how far her influence decided the affair of their hearts.

Shortly after the breakdown of this romance, Madeline married Arthur Walker about whom very little is known. Joe remained a bachelor. After Arthur's death in 1903 Madeline renewed her acquaintance with Joe, corresponding with him and meeting him occasionally until 1914 when Joe married Violet Hay. Violet must have understood the situation because to her credit she continued to write to Madeline in most friendly terms when Joe was no longer able to do so. Strangely enough Joe and Madeline died within a few weeks of one another in 1935.

It seems likely that the romance and its aftermath had affected Madeline more than it did Joe. She was left without her parents and with the responsibility of looking after her young nephews. He had already established himself as an artist and was rapidly gaining a reputation for his works and there would be too much to occupy his mind to meditate for long over his love affair with Madeline. After his father's death when he was thirty, Joe spent more and more of his time at Finzean, painting and enjoying the recreation of the countryside. Life for him and his brother, Robert, was made very comfortable and happy by his stepmother, the beautiful Mary Anne Girdwood. She had looked after Joe in his youth and indeed through much of his life for over fifty years. They were devoted to one another, he frequently painted her portrait and she idolized his work. She was the perfect hostess, entertaining Robert's political friends and Joe's artistic contemporaries both at Finzean and in London. Any thoughts of marriage which would alter the even tenor of this very pleasant life would never have been entertained either by Robert or Joe. So Joseph remained a bachelor during Mary Anne's lifetime and until he was 68 years old.

Six months after Mary Anne's death, in September 1914, Joseph married Violet Evelyn Hay, the youngest daughter of James Tonor Hay of Blackhall. Mary Anne had lived in Finzean House for fifty years (38 years as a widow); Violet excelled Mary Anne's record by living in Finzean House for 57 years (36 years as a widow). Thus for 107 years (all but eighteen months) the two women had lived almost continuously in Finzean House, having a very considerable influence on the estate and on the lives of the six lairds who lived during this period.

*   *   *

The background of Violet's life can explain much of the eccentricity of her character. She was the youngest daughter of James Tonor Hay whose father established a very prosperous rope-making business in Leith from the profits of which he built Blackhall Castle, near Banchory. James Tonor was typical of his time, a wealthy industralist, intolerant and often uncouth, who would make a hard bargain and who led a hard life but who at the same time could occasionally be capable of surprising acts of kindness to his family and his workers. His wife, Annie Maria Atkins, was a truly beautiful woman, quiet and patient and a good understanding mother, indeed a complete contrast to her husband. There were seven children by the marriage, four sons and three daughters. Maude and Reggie, the two of the family whom Violet loved the most, died in their youth under tragic circumstances; the four brothers left the family as quickly as possible to escape the autocratic behaviour of their father, and Ethel, the eldest of the family, and Violet, the youngest, remained at home to look after their parents and the affairs of Blackhall. Ethel would almost certainly have married had it not been for the intervention of her father, but nevertheless she remained the dominant member of the family. She was a woman of great character and although circumstances deprived her of many of the pleasures of life, she managed to keep an incredible sense of humour. Poor Violet withdrew more and more into her shell and became almost a complete recluse, devoting herself to the care of a variety of animals for which she could become utterly possessive.

In her limited way she had known the Farquharsons of Finzean all her life. There would be frequent meetings between the two families; her father would shoot at Finzean and the Farquharson family would come over to Blackhall to attend amateur, and occasionally professional, performances in the small theatre on the estate. It was on such occasions that Joe and Violet met. Despite the age difference which strangely enough is sometimes no barrier, Violet fell deeply in love with Joe and when Joe's stepmother died in March 1914, their engagement was announced almost immediately and they were married very quietly in September of that year. How all this had happened one can only speculate but it is certainly true that Violet wanted desperately to break away from Blackhall and that her love for Joe and the opportunity of living as his wife in Finzean House seemed to be more than sufficient reason for a determined approach on her part. And at the same time Joe was now left alone in Finzean with an ageing brother, without the support of the woman who had cared for him since his youth and no doubt he was most willing to welcome the affectionate advances of a woman very much younger than himself.

The first few years of their married life during the Great War were spent quietly at Finzean but when life returned to normal there were visits to London, galleries and receptions to attend, a new life for Violet which she did not relish but which she loyally and proudly tolerated with her husband. At Finzean they lived very comfortably and entertained quite frequently. Although it was not a large house, there was a staff of five inside and three gardeners outside. One of the surviving members of the staff (engaged at that time at two pounds per month) recalls the annual visits of the whole household to London and later to their house on the west coast. She remembers the kindness and consideration of Robert and Joseph towards the staff but how the whole staff held Violet in some awe. It was her particular duty to wash Joseph's paint brushes with soda and soft soap and if the job was especially well done she would be rewarded with a sixpence.

Towards the end of the twenties Joe had become an old man and his health had been seriously affected by a disabling shooting accident. He died at Finzean in 1935 in his 89th year and was buried in the churchyard at Birse.

*   *   **

Immediately after his death Violet reduced the household and gardening staff, sold their house at Loch Linnhe and again became a recluse, seldom seeing anyone except her sister, her doctor and one or two close friends. Her mother had died three years after Joe, and the family home at Blackhall was sold and eventually demolished, many of the fine granite blocks being transported to London for rebuilding the bomb-damaged Houses of Parliament.

Violet had had an unhappy childhood and much sorrow throughout her life. Her marriage to Joe could have been supremely happy had she been able to give him a child but their failure to produce an heir to Finzean became an obsession with Violet. It was always in her mind that Francis, her father-in-law, had six sons without issue and that her marriage to Joe was the last hope of giving a direct heir to Finzean. But it was not to be. After Joe's death it almost seemed that Violet had little or no interest in the future of Finzean. She lived in the memory of her devoted husband; for years his studio remained as it had been when he painted his last picture, the unfinished canvas still on the easel. Everything had to continue as it had been done in Joe's day. But in 1954 tragedy befell Finzean when the house was almost completely demolished by fire, only the kitchen premises and part of one wing remaining. All her Farquharson pictures and most of the valuables were lost for ever. As she was then a tenant of the house, the fire might have been an opportunity for her to end her tenancy and move elsewhere. But it was her wish to continue to live in the remaining part of the house surrounded by the charred ruins of the old building. However, her wish to retain the ruins had to be overruled and a comfortable and convenient house was rebuilt outwardly in the style of the old house and around that part of the building that had survived the fire. Violet refused even to enter the new house and continued for the remaining seventeen years of her life in the cramped surroundings of the old house. They were sufficient for her needs as she never entertained and seldom saw people other than a few relatives and friends. Yet she managed to retain a deep interest in the people of Finzean, lending her garden to visitors on "open days" and fetes for local charities, always on the clear understanding that she would not be expected to attend. She passed the time driving around the countryside as fast as her car and her chauffeur would allow, she read lots of novels and she enjoyed a flutter on the horses. Until she was no longer able she would spend a day on the hill deer stalking with her keeper, Donald Macleod, a curious contrast to her devoted love of animals and birds.

She died in 1971 at the age of 83 in Finzean House in the room overlooking her garden and the estate, the lady of Finzean for 57 years during the time of five lairds, and she is buried beside her husband in Birse churchyard.

IV

The Family of Joseph Cauvin Farquharson 1806-1860 (brother of Francis Farquharson) and Angelica Erskine 1811-1867

| Angelica Erskine 1837-1892 m. Benjamin Porter Fraser, U.S.A. (our American Cousins)1846-1919 | William Walter 1839-1910 m. Hamilton Belhaven Gillan (The Finzean Succession) | David Erskine 1842-1872 m. Julia ? | Francis Joseph 1848-1912 | James Stirling 1849-1936 | Madeline Margaret 1852-1935 m. Rev. Arthur Walker |

151

6. Joseph Cauvin Farquharson and his Descendants

As there was no direct heir to Finzean in 1935 after Joseph RA died, my uncle, <u>Joseph Gillan Farquharson</u> (Uncle Joe) — a second cousin of Joseph RA — succeeded to the estate and he thus became <u>the thirteenth laird of Finzean</u> (1935-1939). Uncle Joe's grandfather, Joseph Cauvin Farquharson (1806-1860) was the younger brother of Francis, the tenth laird of Finzean, who had done so much in his time to improve the estate.

Joseph Cauvin married Angelica Erskine, the daughter of a successful business man from Langside, Peebles, and they soon became established as a prominent Edinburgh family. Their six children were all born at 13 Pitt Street, later moving to the more elegant property of 9 Inverleith Place. The four boys went to the nearby Edinburgh Academy, joining their cousins, the six sons of Francis. There must have been at one time during the 1850s at least seven Farquharson cousins playing in "the yards" of the Edinburgh Academy. While Francis' family followed the medical profession and produced three generations of Edinburgh doctors, Joseph Cauvin's family chose banking as their career and in their turn produced three generations of Edinburgh bankers. Apart from the two girls, the family were all buried in Warriston Cemetery in Edinburgh.

Joseph Cauvin's children made their contribution to the Farquharson family history. Angelica Erskine (1837-1892) named after her mother and called Ainie by her family, was the eldest of the six children. At the age of 22 she became engaged to Benjamin Porter Fraser, a young American ostensibly studying at the University of Edinburgh but in fact spending much of his time enjoying the social rounds of the capitals of Europe. Angelica's father insisted that he should at least have the prospects of a settled career before marriage, but before this was to be achieved Joseph Cauvin died. Ben soon persuaded his future mother-in-law that his prospects were good and the marriage took place at the family home in Inverleith Place on 17th November 1863. Ben was no sooner married than he returned to America to fight for his State in the American Civil War. For eighteen months he experienced great hardships as a casualty and as a prisoner but after the war as a reward for his services he was decorated with "the Southern Cross of the Legion of Honor".

At home there had been no news of Ben during all this time and it was feared he had been killed in the fighting. However, in August

1865, he returned safely to his wife and to his surprise and delight to a daughter already nearly a year old. Two months later the family moved back to America where Ben was to manage the family property in South Carolina. There were heartrending scenes on the quayside as Angelica's family came to bid them farewell and as it turned out they were never to see her again.

She never returned to her beloved Scotland, devoting the rest of her life to raising a family of nine children in 28 years. She died in 1892 at the age of 55.

Angelica has a significant place in the history of the Farquharson family as seven of her nine children married, each having families of their own and thus the connection with "our American cousins" was established. Most of them now live in North and South Carolina or Virginia.

To trace in any detail our American relations up to the present day becomes almost impossible as their families continued to be large; most of them have married, some of them divorced (often more than once) and some of them have remarried. It is certainly beyond the wit of an amateur genealogist to follow such family connections. But the family connection continues; as recently as 1964 there was christened in Charlotte, North Carolina, a child named Angelica Farquharson Hastings, the great great grand-daughter of Angelia Erskine Farquharson, the niece of Francis Farquharson, the tenth laird of Finzean. Like the first Angelica she is known as Ainie, a family abbreviation continuing for one hundred and fifty years.

Nan (Angelica) Roystone, like myself the great grand-child of Joseph Cauvin Farquharson, now lives in Arlington, USA and maintains a lively interest in her Farquharson relations. She has written a booklet tracing the connections between the Farquharsons of Finzean and their descendants in America and it is from this source that most of this information has been got. The Finzean Farquharsons certainly hope that the link with their "American cousins" will not be forgotten.

*   *   *

My grandfather, <u>William Walter Farquharson</u> (<u>1839-1910</u>) — "Grandfather Farkie" — was the second child of Joseph Cauvin, a man of substantial proportions and few words who at an early age went to India as an indigo planter. After setting up his home in

India, he married Hamilton Belhaven Gillan (1846-1919) — "Granny Farkie" — and there the four children of their family were born. Granny Farkie was the daughter of the Very Reverend Robert Gillan, Moderator of the General Assembly of the Church of Scotland in 1873 and for many years minister of Inchinnan, Renfrewshire. My grandfather must have spent nearly thirty years in India, before returning to Scotland with sufficient means to live comfortably in the family home of 9 Inverleith Place in Edinburgh. When he died in 1910, my grandmother moved to the lower flat of a splendid Georgian house at 69 Great King Street, which became a second home to our family for nearly fifty years. Like his father before him, my grandfather was a staunch Episcopalian while my grandmother, the daughter of a Moderator, was as ardent a Presbyterian as you could wish to find. On Sunday, they would go their different ways, Grandfather Farkie turning to the right as he left 69 Great King Street towards St. George's Episcopal Church accompanied by a reluctant Uncle Joe and an enthusiastic Aunt Angie, while Granny Farkie turned to the left to St. Bernard's Church of Scotland taking with her two of the church's keenest supporters, my mother and Aunt Annie. So far as one knows divided loyalties of denomination created no division in a very happy family.

My sisters remembered Grandfather Farkie as a reserved old gentleman, kindly but ill at ease with children whom he would entertain by making a variety of animal noises even beyond the age when my sisters ceased to find them amusing. Granny Farkie was a women of Victorian virtues which she would expect of her children and grandchildren. She was gracious. She would dress immaculately and to the end of her days would walk erect and with dignity. I picture her sitting upright in her drawing room; indeed she never appeared to sit comfortably in a chair and she would expect her family to follow her example. Yet she was devoted to us all and when we visited her she would embrace us warmly and hold us in the folds of her well corsetted bosom. She and Grandfather Farkie were always honest, and often outspoken in their views, a characteristic which was handed down to their four children. Grandfather Farkie died in 1910 and Granny Farkie nine years later in 1919, and were both buried in Warriston.

*   *   *

Of the four remaining members of Joseph Cauvin's family there is less to record.

David Erskine Farquharson, the third child (1842-1872) married a girl called Julia but they died within months of one another both at the age of 30 and are buried in Warriston, Edinburgh. They left two boys, Henry William Erskine (1864-1929) and Edward Joseph Erskine (1865-1934) who were only seven and eight years of age when their parents died. In their youth they were looked after for several years by their Aunt Madeline, the youngest of Joseph Cauvin's family. When Madeline married the boys were old enough to support themselves and they left her home in Dunblane to follow careers in England. Madeline had been like a mother to them and they never forgot her care and her kindness, frequently visiting her throughout her long life; in fact she outlived them both by a few years. Henry and Edward married two sisters, Edith and Alice Tapper and settled in Southend-on-Sea where they lived for the rest of their lives. Henry and Edith had four daughters, and a grandson named Donald Farquharson Shorter, a very distant cousin of Donald Farquharson, younger, of Finzean. Edward and Alice had one son and no grandchildren. So the Farquharson line from the family of David Erskine Farquharson ended at this point.

Francis Joseph Farquharson, the fourth child (1848-1912) lived part of his life in Edinburgh and latterly at Roberton, Roxburghshire, where he died unmarried. He was a man devoted to good works and spent much of his time tramping the countryside always in his black coat and bowler hat calling from door to door collecting subscriptions for the Edinburgh Royal Infirmary and the mission schemes of the Church of Scotland. He was apparently a genial man with many friends, but without a settled career.

James Stirling, the fifth child (1849-1936) — "Uncle James" — was a very dear friend to the family and particularly to his grand nieces and nephew. Although he was sixty years older than me we struck up a close friendship when I was a boy. We used to walk together on a Sunday afternoon in the Edinburgh Botanic Gardens when he would tell me about his early days at the Edinburgh Academy, how Robert Louis Stevenson was in his class and how he dreamt away the day and was frequently reprimanded for inattention, how he seemed to live more in his imagination than in the hard realities of school life. Uncle James was a Fellow of the Royal Zoological Society. Some of my happiest memories were spent with him in visits to the zoo and the afternoon completed with a sumptuous tea in the Fellows' dining room. Several times we went to the early silent cinema together which I think he enjoyed almost as much as I did. Unfortunately I saw little of him in his latter years but the memory of his friendship I shall always cherish. He was a bachelor, living comfortably in the Murrayfield area of Edinburgh and cared for with great devotion by Christina, his housekeeper. He had been a banker all his life, finishing his career as the manager (then called "the agent") of the West End Branch of the National Bank of Scotland in Edinburgh. He died in 1936 and is buried in Warriston, Edinburgh.

The sixth and youngest child of Joseph Cauvin was <u>Madeline Margaret</u> (<u>1852-1935</u>) — "Aunt Maddie". Born in Edinburgh, she was only eight when her father died and fifteen when her mother died and it seems that in her youth she was looked after by a lady by the name of Christian who was probably an aunt on the Erskine side of the family. With the premature death of her parents, the heavy responsibilities of looking after two orphan nephews and the heart breaking romance with her cousin Joe, the early life of Madeline had not been easy. At the age of 26 she married in London the Reverend Arthur Walker, a Church of England clergyman. Shortly after this marriage, Arthur Walker became vicar of the attractive parish of Wethersfield, Essex, where three of their four children were born. Bringing up a family in a large vicarage on a small stipend was a struggle for Arthur and Maddie, but despite the hardships of their upbringing their family flourished and three (Robert Farquharson, Mary Angelica and Dora Veronica) of the four children married. Emily Madeline, the unmarried daughter, continued to live with her mother. Arthur Walker died at the age of 58 leaving Aunt Maddie a widow for over 30 years in very straitened circumstances. Her husband had left little to support her and such family inheritance as there had been had dwindled away to almost nothing. She could expect little help from her elder brothers and sister as they had married and gone abroad; of her two unmarried brothers Uncle Frank could give no support as he himself depended almost entirely on his share of the modest family inheritance and was really incapable of supplementing it by his own wits, while it was left to Uncle James to give such support as he could to his sister, our grand aunt Maddie, from his salary and pension from the National Bank of Scotland. Madeline died in 1935 and is buried beside her husband in Kingston, Surrey.

Although Madeline's family and their descendants have lived

almost entirely in the south of England they have retained their Scottish connection by keeping the name Farquharson in their family. Three of her great grandsons are Farquharson Smiths, one grandson, two great-grandsons and two great-great-grandsons are Farquharson Harts; one Stuart Richard Farquharson Hart, born in 1977, is one of the Farquharsons of Finzean. It is to Peggy Hart, like me a great grandchild of Joseph Cauvin Farquharson, that I am indebted for much of the information she has provided about this side of our family.

*   *   *

Joseph Gillan Farquharson (1867-1938) — "Uncle Joe" — was the only son of William Walter Farquharson and a second cousin of Joseph Farquharson, RA whom he succeeded in 1935 as the thirteenth laird of Finzean (1935-1938). He was born in India but returned as a boy to be educated at the Edinburgh Institution (now Melville College). The influence of his uncle, James Stirling, who was already well established in the National Bank of Scotland, no doubt guided Uncle Joe into banking as a career. He would certainly have been described as a very sound and reliable banker but he was too shy and retiring to seek higher position in the profession, ending his career as manager of one of the Perth branches of the National Bank.

Like all the Farquharsons of his generation, he was an exceedingly courteous man and would judge people more by their manners than any other qualities. He would dress immaculately and as expensively as his purse would allow, his infrequent visits to London being made for no other purpose than to see his tailor. He enjoyed the company of a small circle of male friends with whom he would meet regularly in the historic Royal Perth Golf Club. There was nothing he enjoyed more than a golfing holiday or a fortnight's fishing on the Dee although he never fished on the Finzean water. He was a very good family man, taking a great interest in the welfare of his sisters and his nieces and nephew, forever showing acts of thoughtfulness and generosity towards them. Although he was a confirmed bachelor he was not unmoved by feminine charm and there may have been some truth in the charge made by his sisters that Joe was "a dark horse". But he enjoyed his bachelor existence far too much to change his ways in later life, living as he did in a delightful flat in Perth overlooking the River Tay and being cared for with great devotion by a faithful housekeeper.

So when he became laird of Finzean at the age of 68, he had no wish to move north and settle on the estate; in fact, inheritance to him was a burden rather than a benefit. It was a burden because he had inherited an estate which was heavily bonded, which had to pay annually to the surviving widow of Joseph RA a proportion of the rents of the tenanted property, and in addition there were substantial Estate Duties to be met. And it was a worry because there was no money in the estate to meet those obligations, and Uncle Joe could not provide funds from his own resources. Nor could he sell property from the estate because of the entail which prohibited any sale from Finzean, Lumphanan or Migvie. The first step was to free the estate of the restraints of the entail and this was affected after lengthy legal procedures by an Instrument of Disentail dated 19th February 1936, thus breaking an entail which had held Finzean for 152 years during the lives of eight lairds. It was now possible to sell Lumphanan and Migvie (about 8000 acres) for a sum of about £25,000, sufficient to meet the Estate Duties and to provide a modest sum for investment to support the Estate.

All these worries came upon Uncle Joe when he was enjoying a well-earned retirement. There is no doubt this had an effect upon his health, heart attacks became more frequent and he died very suddenly at the age of 71, a laird for three years who had no roots in Finzean, who never spent a night on the estate and visited it as seldom as possible. Yet during those three years he left Finzean free of debt, he changed the legal position of the estate and halved its boundaries, and consequently altered the line of succession of the lairds.

*   *   *

Uncle Joe had three sisters. The eldest, <u>Annie Charlotte Erskine</u> (<u>1865-1944</u>) — "Aunt Annie" — returned from India in her early twenties and lived with her family in Edinburgh where she remained for the rest of her life, at 52 Inverleith Row, at 69 Great King Street and at 22 Dundas Street. She remained unmarried and as a maiden aunt she became the benefactor of our family. There was always a warm welcome to her house and we would stay with her sometimes for long periods while we were at school or at college. My parents had limited means to bring up a family of four, my father having no more than his modest stipend while my mother supplemented this with a very small private income, so the assistance which Aunt Annie was so glad to give was often more than welcome. I stayed with her for four years, two years while I was at school and two years as a student at Edinburgh University. Although I was unaware of it at the time, those were years when the family income could not afford the boarding fees at school and at college, and Aunt Annie had come to the rescue. Looking back on this time nearly sixty years later, the formative years I spent with her taught me more than I would ever have learnt in a boarding establishment.

Her benefactions were not limited to the family as she was a tireless worker in support of good causes. As a devoted member of the Church of Scotland, her Sunday was no day of rest. She would be in her pew at St. Bernards regularly at both morning and evening services and would teach in the Bible class in the afternoon. During the week she would dispense soup to the poor at the Edinburgh Shelter in the Canongate, help in the activities of the Society for the Prevention of Cruelty to Children, hold Shakesperian readings in her drawing room during the winter evenings and attend a programme of lectures run by the Edinburgh Philosophical Society, a less elevated body than the title would suggest. As if all this was not enough, she was an active supporter of the Conservative Unionist Party. Staying with her was certainly an education in itself. She taught me to be a regular church attender although she would not expect attendance more than once a Sunday; she would describe to me the poverty and distress she had seen in the slums of Edinburgh and she introduced me to politics which for me became a lifelong interest. The first political meeting I attended as the age of eleven had almost a Dickensian atmosphere; a small packed smokey schoolroom in Stockbridge charged with political animosity, and sitting in the front row Aunt Annie and me. She was always first at any meeting, "to be sure of getting a seat". As the back rows shouted down the candidate, Aunt Annie would threaten them with her umbrella and arouse even further abuse. When I grew a little older we would canvass for the party and would be given part of a street in which to distribute literature and solicit support. On one occasion at a by-election in Leith, our assignment was to cover a tenement area and as the younger member of the team I was better able to climb the stairs and canvass the higher flats. It seemed that the higher the tenancies in this dockland area the lower was the virtue of their occupants and this young Academy boy soon found he was greeted alternately with terms of mock endearment and with improper abuse, a lively introduction to politics and the realities of life.

Aunt Annie died in 1944. When life had become very difficult in Edinburgh during the War, she spent her last two years with my parents in Gifford, East Lothian. They must have been so pleased to give a final home to this dear, compassionate lady who had been so kind to us all throughout her life.

*   *   *

Mary Eleanor (1871-1954) — my mother, called Nora by her family — was Uncle Joe's second and younger sister. Although six years younger than Aunt Annie they shared common characteristics, similar interests and were very close to one another. They both had a brusque and forthright Scottish manner, and were impatient of anything they regarded as nonsense. In running their houses they were economical and thrifty, indeed my mother who always kept the family accounts was obliged to be thrifty bringing up a family of four on a very small income. From the earliest age we were brought up to understand the limits of the family budget and we asked for no more. We were well educated in the less expensive Edinburgh schools and our holidays were spent happily but simply within the bounds of Scotland, usually in some country manse where my father would take services for a month during the summer, but always finding time with his family to enjoy walking, fishing and golf. We were not a difficult family in any respect, but even the best mannered families have their problems and in our case my mother would always meet these problems with calm deliberation. Whatever she may have felt inwardly my mother never appeared to be upset although there was certainly cause to be at times as my father could be intolerant and occasionally quick tempered. Looking back on my youth, my mother ran the family extremely well with an affection and a quiet orderliness which was so valuable in our upbringing. We were expected to be diligent, tidy, punctual and well-mannered but if these qualities tended towards priggishness, such a tendency was quickly scorned and condemned by my parents.

After his graduation my father became assistant minister to the celebrated Dr. Matheson, minister of St. Bernard's Church in Edinburgh where my mother was an enthusiastic member of the congregation. They must have met frequently at church functions and no doubt my mother would have been attracted by this tall handsome young minister as he would have been by the vivacious Nora Farquharson. They became engaged before my father went to his first parish in Old Meldrum, Aberdeenshire in 1895, and were married the following year. Hannah, my eldest sister, was born two years later in the south-west bedroom of the manse of Old Meldrum, the same room where the rest of the family were born.

My father moved to St. John's Church, Dundee, in 1909. Ten years in Dundee were the most difficult in my mother's life. For four years before the outbreak of the Great War in 1914, the family were growing up and needed constant attention, my father and mother were settling into the new work of a city parish, there was great activity in the raising of funds for the building of a fine new church and my mother devoted herself wholeheartedly in support of this great enterprise of her husband, the young minister of the parish. At the outbreak of war my father became a chaplain and was away from the family for the best part of four years leaving my mother to shoulder responsibilities in the running of the parish and to care for her young family. Conditions in the manse at this time were very difficult. The limited family income was further depleted by hospitality to be given to visiting ministers and in addition there was much deprivation caused by the war. I can recall such strain and anxiety within the family that for the first and only time I saw my mother distressed.

Shortly after the war we moved to Whittingehame, East Lothian, which was a haven of peace after wartime Dundee. My mother made the beautiful manse a very happy home for us all and she and my father worked hard in the garden. Some small legacies improved the family income and my parents were now able to employ the diminutive Jimmie Boyd to help in the garden and the contrastingly ample Maggie to be a maid of all work in the house. The crowning year of my father's ministry was 1935 when he became Moderator of the General Assembly of the Church of Scotland. My mother was his proud and able consort throughout a very busy year and she and Aunt Annie attended every session of the Assembly, following the debates with well informed interest.

My mother was in her seventieth year when my father retired to an attractive house in its own grounds in Gifford, East Lothian, about eight miles from Whittingehame. There they spent fifteen years of happy retirement near their friends, working in their garden and occasionally visiting Edinburgh. Mother continued to have a great interest and devotion for her family until the day of her death. All her family were now married and were scattered around the world. Hannah was for some time in India and latterly in England; Laurina, as an army officer's wife, moved around the world, and I was in the Sudan. Eleanor was the only one who lived near home, a few miles from Dunbar. The arrival of the post with the possibility of a letter from one of the family was the great event of their day. When a letter arrived, all work was set aside. My father would settle down in his chair and light his pipe while my mother often with pride and emotion would read out the letter, to be read again in the evening and discussed throughout the week. Mother died very suddenly in her chair in front of the fire, at the age of 82, a great shock to my father but a blessing that the end had come so quickly and without undue distress. My mother is buried in Whittingehame churchyard.

*   *   *

Madeline Angelique (1876-1957) — "Aunt Angie" or "Tangie" to the younger members of the family — spent the early years of her life in Edinburgh, but as she grew up she became more independent of the family. Unlike most girls of her circumstances at that time she was trained as a secretary but during the first World War she worked as a nurse in a military hospital in Edinburgh and for a short time in France. She was a staunch Episcopalian and was a regular attender and helper at St.Mary's Cathedral, Edinburgh. It was while she was working in a mission there that she met William Shuckburgh Swayne — "Uncle Toby" — at that time Vicar of St. Peter's, Cranley Gardens, London. Uncle Toby's first wife had died in 1916 and in the following year he married Aunt Angie. She was 41 when they were married and he was 15 years older. Uncle Toby was typical of his time, as broad in his theology as he was in his physique, full of good humour, confidence and ambition, with endless stories of Oxford and achievements on river, but at the same time very much a man of God, friendly to all persons, an inspiring preacher delivering his message with great Christian assurance. He moved from St. Peter's to become Dean of Manchester and in 1920 was consecrated Bishop of Lincoln where he continued until he retired in 1932 at the age of 70.

Uncle Toby and Aunt Angie were a formidable team in Lincoln. They were both positive characters and would dominate the scene at

The Bishop of Lincoln and Aunt Angie.

any gathering. Uncle Toby was regarded as an excellent administrator whose authority in the diocese was never to be challenged and Aunt Angie was his loyal accomplice. He probably made the mistake of allowing Aunt Angie the responsibility of running the clerical side of his office, giving her access to the confidences of the diocese and perhaps with some justification this earned her the nickname amongst the less respectful clergy and laity of "the Lincoln Handicap".

To the whole family Uncle Toby and Aunt Angie were very kind, making the Old Palace at Lincoln open house to my sisters and myself and later when they retired to 69 Great King Street, Edinburgh, we were always welcome. Uncle Toby died in 1941 and Aunt Angie continued to live in "69" for the remaining sixteen years of her life, taking an active part in church and other affairs. To the end of her days she was a formidable person. Anyone who had the temerity to challenge her opinion would be met with a stoney silence or an abrupt remark to end all discussion. Yet beneath this brusque and outspoken manner, she had the kindest heart and would spare no effort to help a friend or a member of the family who had met with some misfortune. She would have a very shrewd appreciation of any situation and her opinions were always to be valued.

She died in the summer of 1957 and is buried beside Uncle Toby in the Farquharson family burial ground in Warriston Cemetery, Edinburgh.

*   *   *

When Joseph Gillan Farquharson (Uncle Joe) died in 1938, the estate of Finzean having been disentailed during his years as laird, it was no longer obligatory for succession to follow the rule of primogeniture. Accordingly Uncle Joe bequeathed the estate to me as his only nephew. There arose immediately the question of my name. When I succeeded to the estate one of my Christian names was Farquharson and my surname was Lang. As the Laird of Finzean had been a Farquharson of Finzean since the sixteenth century, there was pressure upon me by the Lord Lyon, Sir Thomas Innes of Learney, Mrs. Violet Farquharson and others to drop the name of Lang and take the name of Farquharson of Finzean. On the other hand I was most anxious as one of the two male survivors of our distinguished branch of the Lang family to retain the paternal name of Lang. So a compromise was reached and I became William Marshall Farquharson-Lang, the 14th Laird of Finzean (1938-1961).

I continued as laird until 1961 when my only daughter, Alison Mary, married and on her marriage I gifted to her the estate of Finzean. Her husband, Angus Miller, graciously agreed to take the name of Farquharson and my daughter as the new laird of Finzean became Alison Mary Farquharson, the 15th Laird of Finzean (1961-) thus resuming the feudal barony and the high honour of the arms and supporters of the Farquharsons of Finzean.

7. The Farquharson Chieftainship

The Lord Lyon King of Arms first awarded the Chieftainship of the Farquharson Clan to Farquharson of Invercauld in 1815 and since then the decision of the Lord Lyon at that time has been confirmed by his successors in 1938 and as recently as 1949, some years after the present laird of Invercauld, Captain Farquharson (formerly Alwyne Arthur Compton), inherited the estate under the settlement of his maternal grandfather, Lieutenant Colonel Alexander Haldane Farquharson, the 14th Laird of Invercauld. Myrtle Farquharson, the elder of the two daughters of Alexander Farquharson, had resumed her maiden name on marriage when she succeeded her father as 15th Laird of Invercauld. She was laird from 1936 to 1941 when she was killed in an air raid on London. Captain Farquharson, Myrtle's nephew and elder son of her younger sister, Sylvia, then became the 16th Laird of Invercauld and it was to him in 1946 that the Lord Lyon most recently confirmed the chieftainship of the clan.

The Farquharsons of Finzean have from time to time questioned the award of the chieftainship to Invercauld. Finzean has maintained that if the chieftainship was awarded on grounds of primogeniture, Finzean would have a prior claim. Their case goes back to the time of Finla Mor, the first laird of Invercauld, the father of Donald Farquharson of Tillygarmond and the grandfather of Robert Farquharson, the first laird of Finzean. Finla Mor had two wives, four children by his first wife and ten, at least, by his second wife. There is evidence to support the Finzean claim that it is from a senior branch of this large family that the Finzean inheritance stems, but it must be admitted there is some dubiety in this claim. Family records and family relationships in the seventeenth century were to say the least often unreliable and irregular. To quote a letter on the subject written in 1950, the Lord Lyon wrote,

> "In those days one is never very certain what ongoings were afoot in the house of a Highland Chief, of whom the English barrister, Mr. A.C. Foxe-Davies, once issued the acid and weary comment that it was sometimes difficult to say which, if any, of the ladies in the household of a Highland Chief could be dignified with the name of his wife. There is considerable doubt about the maternity of Finla Mor's progeny."

The crux of the matter was not so much who was the heir-male that could claim the chieftainship of the clan, but rather who held the inheritance of the ancient family estate, "the hearth of the race". Invercauld had certainly been the family "hearth" long before the Farquharsons acquired the lands of Finzean and it was the fact that the Invercauld Farquharsons had continuously occupied the estate to the present day that was the principal, or at any rate the most material, point that determined the award of the Chieftainship of the Clan Farquharson.

No doubt the debate will continue to fascinate future genealogists, but as time passes the title of chieftain has less significance in a modern world and may eventually become an interesting relic of Scottish clan history.

The Lairds of Finzean

1. 1609-1632   Robert Farquharson,
                son of Donald Farquharson of Tillygarmond
2. 1638-1666   Alexander Farquharson
                son of 1
3. 1666-1707   Francis Farquharson
                son of 2
4. 1707-1742   Robert Farquharson
                son of 3
5. 1742-1786   Francis Farquharson
                son of 4
6. 1786   Francis Farquharson
                cousin of 5 and grandson of 4
7. 1786-1796   Archibald Farquharson
                son of 6
8. 1796-1841   Archibald Farquharson
                son of 7
9. 1841-1849   John Farquharson
                uncle of 8 and son of 6
10. 1849-1876   Francis Farquharson
                distant cousin of 9 and great (×3) grandson of 2
11. 1876-1918   Robert Farquharson
                son of 10
12. 1918-1935   Joseph Farquharson
                brother of 11
13. 1935-1938   Joseph Gillan Farquharson
                second cousin of 12 and grand nephew of 10
14. 1938-1961   William Marshall Farquharson-Lang
                nephew of 13
15. 1961-   Alison Mary Farquharson
                daughter of 14

Family Forecast

This history of the two families — the Langs and Farquharsons — spans roughly a period of two hundred years — 1750 to 1950 — and has attempted to describe the lives and careers of the families during five or six generations. Those who had lived at the beginning of the period could not have foreseen how their descendants would have lived two hundred years later and those who had lived at the end of the period would find it difficult to imagine how their ancestors had tolerated the conditions of life two hundred years earlier. According to the standards of their times they lived modestly and comfortably. In modern parlance they were middle class folk. In spite of their large families there was no poverty, they lived in houses of moderate size and they accepted the standards of education of their times and in their achievements fulfilled the opportunities they had been given. They were ardently Scottish but at the same time they were staunch upholders of the Union. Although some of them, like so many Scots, had pursued a career abroad, often in international banking, in their later years they usually returned to their homeland and were glad and proud to retain their Scottish inheritance.

Both families had made some small but at times significant contribution to the history of Scotland and sometimes beyond its boundaries, the Langs largely within the sphere of the church and the Farquharsons in the development of land ownership. The Langs were strongly Presbyterian, with roots going back to the stormy times of the Covenanters progressing onward to the quieter ecumenical trends of present day Scotland. There was a time during the latter half of the nineteenth century after the Disruption when the profession of the Langs was predominantly in the ministry of the Church of Scotland and many parishes were glad to welcome into their community a Lang as their minister. Although the early years of the twentieth century saw some deviation from Presbyterianism with Cosmo at Canterbury and Norman at Leicester and Peterborough, strangely enough although by intellectual and spiritual conversion Cosmo and Norman could not accept the tenets of Presbyterianism there was in both of them a strong bond towards the Presbyterian outlook and a deep regard for the church of their father.

At the risk of invidious comparison John Marshall (1834-1909) should be regarded as the finest member of the Lang family.

Although he did not hit the headlines achieved by his son, Cosmo, there was so much in his life of which his family could be proud. The father of eight children, some of whom reached high distinction, a minister of the church of great devotion labouring for twenty-seven years in Glasgow to improve the social conditions of the people, and a central figure in nineteenth century public life.

The fortunes of the Farquharsons fluctuated to a greater degree. The estate of Finzean reached its lowest ebb at the end of the eighteenth and into the first half of the nineteenth century during the lairdships of Archibald and John Farquharson, but it is to Francis Farquharson (1802-1876) that credit must be given for the revival of its status. While he was laird (1849-1876) he improved beyond all recognition the farming and forestry of the estate and converted the hovels of the people within the estate into the acceptable housing conditions of the time. He was the father of six sons, but regrettably the grandfather of none. Although his son, Joseph, by his paintings gained an international reputation, it must be to Francis that the Farquharson accolade is awarded.

There are too many imponderables in the calculation to attempt to extrapolate the progress of the family into the twenty-first century. Unfortunately for Scotland the Langs have tended to move south of the border and to become anglicized, eight of the eleven grandchildren of John Marshall Lang having settled outside the boundaries of the country of their origin, accountably because of marriage, the Oxbridge factor and the greater opportunities that have lured them away from Scotland. Perhaps future generations will remember with some pride that their origins stem from a distinguished Scottish family. The Farquharsons on the other hand remain in Finzean and so long as political and economic conditions allow, they will continue to do so.

*   *   *